WRITING CONVERSATIONAL KOREAN

Created by Katarina Pollock and Chelsea Guerra
Illustrated by Yujin Kim

GOOSE APPLE
BOOKS

Copyright © 2021 Gooseapple Books, LLC

All rights reserved. No part of this book may be reproduced or used in any manner without the prior written permission of the copyright owner, except for the use of brief quotations in a book review.
To request permissions, please contact: support@gooseapplebooks.com

Paperback ISBN: 978-1-7376777-0-3

First paperback edition: September 2021

Translations by 강은영
Edited by 박정민 and 이에니
Illustrations by 김유진

QR Codes to all YouTube videos included with video owner's permission
Excerpts Reprinted by Permission: Native writing samples voluntarily submitted by anonymous users with knowledge of their submission's purpose.

www.gooseapplebooks.com

– THE COMPLETE –
WRITING CONVERSATIONAL KOREAN SERIES

 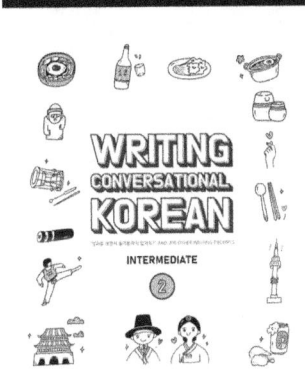 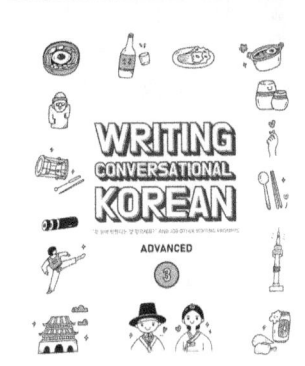 

Writing Conversational Korean: Book One
" 코를 골아요?"
and 200 other writing prompts

Chapters
Experiences, Abilities, Habits, Travel

Korean Level
Intermediate +

Writing Conversational Korean: Book Two
"영화를 보면서 울어 본 적이 있어요?"
and 200 other writing prompts

Chapters
Preferences, Entertainment, Food, Nature

Korean Level
Intermediate +

Writing Conversational Korean: Book Three
"첫 눈에 반한다는 걸 믿으세요?"
and 200 other writing prompts

Chapters
Family, Feelings, Desires, Relationships, Friends

Korean Level
Advanced +

Writing Conversational Korean: Book Four
"당신은 외계인을 믿으세요?"
and 200 other writing prompts

Chapters
Memories, Personality, Opinions, Work, School

Korean Level
Advanced +

For more information, check out the books on our website.
www.gooseapplebooks.com/books

A big
thank you
to all the people who
contributed to this book.

Thank you to 강은영 for translating and
to 박정민 and 이에니 for help proof-reading

Thank you to all the YouTubers who allowed
us to share their videos in this book

And a big thank you to all the people who
submitted responses to our surveys,
particularly /r/hanguk!

정말 감사합니다

Table of Contents

00 - 이 책의 활용법 - How to use this book 8

1A - 경험에 대한 질문 - Questions about experiences 18
    GRAMMAR FORM : ~(으)ㄴ가요?/~나요? 19
    GRAMMAR FORM : ~(으)ㄴ 적이 있다/없다 20
    VIDEO : 크루즈 여행 두번 해보고 느낀 솔직 장단점 [book Q: Have you ever ridden on a boat?] 41
    VIDEO : SNS를 끊고 생긴 4가지 변화 [book Q: Have you ever taken a break from social media? 50
    Would you want to?]

1B - 경험에 대한 원어민 답변예시 - Native Korean Writing Samples 52

2A - 능력에 대한 질문 - Questions about abilities 72
    GRAMMAR FORM : ~을/를 수 있다/없다 73
    GRAMMAR FORM : ~을/를 줄 알다/모르다 74
    VIDEO : FLEX도 습관? 대학생의 통장 털기 [book Q: How financially responsible are you?] 88

2B - 능력에 대한 원어민 답변예시 - Native Korean Writing Samples 90

3A - 습관에 대한 질문 - Questions about habits 106
    GRAMMAR FORM : ~을/를 때 107
    GRAMMAR FORM : ~(으)ㄴ/는 편이다 108
    VIDEO : 연애보다 헬스?! 남녀가 운동에 미친 이유 [book Q: Do you exercise? If so, how?] 112
    VIDEO : 남녀가 안경을 벗으면 달라지는 이유 [book Q: Do you need glasses? Do you want to wear 123
    glasses?]

3B - 습관에 대한 원어민 답변예시 - Native Korean Writing Samples 132

4A - 여행에 대한 질문 - Questions about travel 150

    VIDEO : 당신이 서울에서 꼭 가봐야 할 장소 10 150

    GRAMMAR FORM : ~고 싶다 151

    GRAMMAR FORM : ~(으)려고 하다 152

    VIDEO : [국내여행] 열려라 바닷길!!! 두 발로 직접 바다를 건너다~! 진도 신비의 바닷길 축제 [book Q: Talk..... 153
    about a time you've gone to a festival or a carnival.]

4B - 여행에 대한 원어민 답변예시 - Native Korean Writing Samples 170

05 - 번역 - Translations 188

06 - 어휘 - Word Bank 204

이 책의 활용법

HOW TO USE THIS BOOK

00 활용법

Welcome!

This book contains contains four main components.

Grammar Pages
Pages with a grammar form recommended for use in that chapter. Before you answer any questions, you can watch a video teaching the grammar form in Korean, check the example sentences, and then challenge yourself to utilize the grammar later in your answers.

Question Pages
Pages with writing prompts, and space to write your answers. At the bottom of each question page you may find useful vocabulary words. Use them to help you expand your answers.

Korean Video Pages
Some full page questions may contain a video of native Korean people talking or vlogging about something related to the question in your book. Watch these videos for practice with listening comprehension, new vocab in context, and inspiration for your answers.

Native Korean Writing Samples
For each chapter, 5 questions were selected for native Korean volunteers to respond to. Use their answers for reading practice, reinforce vocab through context, familiarize yourself with native Korean sentence patterns and expressions. English translations of these responses can be found in Chapter 6 (번역).

We hope you enjoy practicing with **Writing Conversational Korean!**

All videos linked in the book are present with the consent of the video owner. Each response is written by a Korean person with their own opinions, beliefs, and personal history. Any opinion or belief expressed by that individual is a representation of their own thoughts, and not of the makers of this book.

Grammar Pages

~(으)ㄴ 적이 있다/없다

← Name of the grammar form

TO TALK ABOUT THINGS YOU'VE EXPERIENCED IN THE PAST

WATCH A VIDEO LESSON!
Video: Let's learn about 'V-(으)ㄴ 적이 있다/없다' in korean grammar. [ENG CHN sub]
Channel: 꼬미스쿨 GGOMI SCHOOL
TOPIK: 3급 (중급)

QR code linking to the video

Brief grammar explanation

This grammar form can be attached to action verbs (동사)
- Use ~은 적이 있다/없다 if the action verb (동사) ends in a final consonant (받침)
- Use ~ㄴ 적이 있다/없다 if the action verb (동사) does not end in a final consonant
- Use ~(으)ㄴ 적이 있다 to talk about things you have experienced in the past.
- Use ~(으)ㄴ 적이 없다 to talk about things you haven't experienced in the past.

Example sentences in Korean

자전거를 탄 적이 있어요?	Have you ever ridden a bicycle?
한국에 산 적이 없어요.	I have never lived in Korea.
만약에 그 것을 한 적이 없으면 조심하세요.	If you've never done this before, please be careful.
김치를 먹어 본 적이 있어요?	Have you ever eaten kimchi?
네, 먹어 본 적이 있는데 매웠어요.	Yes I have tried it, but it was spicy.

Grammar use highlighted / *English translation*

Question Pages

00 활용법

Question written in Korean
Question written in English

헌혈해 본 적이 있나요?
Have you ever tried donating blood?

Space to write an answer

총을 쏴 본 적이 있나요?
Have you ever tried shooting a gun?

명상을 해 본 적이 있나요?
Have you ever tried meditation?

Potentially useful vocabulary

헌혈 운동 a blood drive | 혈액형 blood type | 사격장 a gun range | (총으로) 표적을 겨누다 to take aim at a target (with a gun) | 마음을 새롭게 하다 to freshen your mind | 평화를 찾다 to find peace | 중심을 잡다 to keep one's balance | 스트레스를 풀다 to relieve stress |

11

Korean Video Pages

Question related to the video

배를 타 본 적이 있나요?
Have you ever ridden on a boat?

Space to write your own answer

QR Code takes you to the YouTube video

Video title Korean & English

LISTEN TO NATIVE SPEAKERS!

Video: 크루즈 여행 두번 해보고 느낀 솔직 장단점 A to Z
We went on two cruises: our honest thoughts on the advantages and disadvantages from A to Z

Channel: 잼쏭부부 jemissong — *YouTube Channel Name*

Level: 중급 (Intermediate) — *Korean language level used in the video*

Vocabulary that appears in the video

예약하다 to book, to reserve | 일정을 짜다 to make a schedule | 장점 advantage | 단점 disadvantage | 파도가 세다 to have strong waves | 멀미 motion sickness | 해협 a straight/channel | 망망대해 the open sea | 햇살 sunshine | 선내 on-board |

'Native Korean Writing Samples' Pages — 00 활용법

대회에서 우승한 적이 있나요?
Have you ever won a contest?

미술대회에 나가서 몇 차례 상을 <mark>받은 적이 있어요.</mark>

↑ Grammar form introduced in the chapter, highlighted

↘ Question asked in the book

대회에서 우승한 적이 있나요?
Have you ever won a contest?

아뇨ㅠ 학교에서 했던 게임 대회 마저 우승 해본적 없는 사람입니다.. 언젠가는 꼭 해보고 싶네요!! ㅋㅋㅋㅋ

↑ Response written by a native Korean speaker

대회에서 우승한 적이 있나요?
Have you ever won a contest?

나는 어렸을 때 피아노를 쳤었어. 피아노 학원을 다니면서 같이 배우는 친구들과 함께 지역 또는 국내 대회에 나가서 상을 <mark>받은 적이 있었지.</mark> 한 곡에 많은 시간과 노력을 들여서 짧은 순간에 평가 받는 일은 쉽지 않은 일이야. 자기 순서를 기다리는 것도 스트레스 받지. 하지만 친구들과 함께 경연에 나가서 내 차례를 기다리면서 마인드 컨트롤 할 수 있었어. 나를 도와 준 선생님과 친구들에게 감사해.

육하원칙: WWWWWH

When answering questions, use 육하원칙 so that you can fill up as much space as possible.

육하원칙: 누구 (who), 언제 (when), 어디서 (where), 무엇 (what), 왜 (why), 어떻게 (how).

For example:

한국에 가 본 적이 있어요?
Have you ever been to Korea?

1. **누구**: 친구들이랑 같이 한국에 갔어요.

2. **언제**: 2018년에 한국에 갔어요.

3. **어디서**: 한국에 갔을 때 서울에 가 봤어요.

4. **무엇**: 맛있는 음식을 많이 먹어 봤어요. 그 중에 가장 맛있는 음식은 삼겹살이었어요.

5. **왜**: 여행하러 한국에 가 봤어요.

6. **어떻게**: 드라마를 보고 한국에 관심이 생겼어요.

Put them all together when writing a response.

한국에 가 본 적이 있어요?
Have you ever been to Korea?

네, 있어요. 2018년에 친구랑 같이 한국에 갔어요. 드라마를 보고 한국에 관심이 생겼었거든요. 한국에서 여행을 하고 싶어서 한국에 가 봤어요. 서울에 가서 맛있는 음식을 많이 먹어 봤어요. 그 중에 가장 맛있는 음식은 삼겹살이었어요.

00 활용법

Another example:

한국어를 배워 본 적이 있어요?
Have you ever tried learning Korean?

1. 누구: 보통 혼자서 공부하고 가끔 친구랑 같이 공부해요.
2. 언제: 올해 한국어를 배우기 시작했어요.
3. 어디서: 보통 우리 집에서 공부하는데 가끔 카페에서 공부해요.
4. 무엇: 어휘와 문법을 공부하고 있어요.
5. 왜: 저는 BTS를 좋아해서 한국어를 배우고 싶어요.
6. 어떻게: 드라마를 보고 음악을 들어요.

Put them all together when writing a response.

한글을 배워 본 적이 있어요?
Have you ever tried learning Korean?

네, 지금 한국어를 배우고 있어요. 저는 BTS를 좋아해서 한국어를 배우고 싶어요. 올해부터 한국어를 배우기 시작했고 어휘와 문법을 공부하고 있어요. 보통 혼자서 우리 집에서 공부하는데 가끔 카페에서 공부하기도 하고 친구랑 함께 공부하기도 해요.

15

활용법 00

Getting Feedback

If you wish to get feedback on what you've written, here are three free options for you to try.

HELLOTALK

"Native speakers teach you their language while you teach them yours. Chat with language partners via text, voice recordings, voice calls, and video calls. Built-in aids for translation, pronunciation, transliteration, and correction make conversation run smoothly."

HINATIVE

"HiNative is a global Q&A platform for language learners. Ask and answer questions about language and culture with native speakers around the world."

/R/WRITESTREAKKOREAN

Post something every day on this reddit forum to build your writing streak.

00 활용법

Further Questions?

Feel free to email us at:

support@gooseapplebooks.com

Keep up to date

SIGN UP TO OUR MAILING LIST ON OUR WEBSITE

And get notified of future updates, including when we release new books.

1A 경험에 대한 질문
QUESTIONS ABOUT EXPERIENCES

문법

~(으)ㄴ가요?/~나요?

TO MAKE QUESTIONS SOFTER AND LESS DIRECT

WATCH A VIDEO LESSON!
Video: **Learn Korean | Korean Grammar 96: A은가요?/ㄴ가요?, V나요?, N인가요?**
Channel: 베이직 코리안 Basic Korean
TOPIK: 2급 (초급)

This grammar form can only be added to questions
- Use ~나요? if the sentence ending is an action verb (동사) (including 있다/없다)
- Use ~(으)ㄴ가요? if the sentence ending is a descriptive verb (형용사)
- Use ~은가요? if the descriptive verb ends in a final consonant (받침)
- Use ~ㄴ가요? if the descriptive verb does not end in a final consonant (받침)
- Use ~인가요? if the sentence ending is a noun (명사)

아침에 운동하나요?	Do you work out in the morning?
김치를 먹을 수 있나요?	Can you eat kimchi?
김치가 매운가요?	Is kimchi spicy?
요즘은 바쁜가요?	Are you busy these days?
미국 사람인가요?	Are you American?
그 음식은 돼지고기인가요?	Is that food pork?

문법

~(으)ㄴ 적이 있다/없다

TO TALK ABOUT THINGS YOU'VE EXPERIENCED IN THE PAST

WATCH A VIDEO LESSON!
Video: Let's learn about 'V-(으)ㄴ 적이 있다/없다' in korean grammar. [ENG CHN sub]
Channel: 꼬미스쿨 GGOMI SCHOOL
TOPIK: 3급 (중급)

This grammar form can be attached to action verbs (동사)
    Use ~은 적이 있다/없다 if the action verb (동사) ends in a final consonant (받침)
    Use ~ㄴ 적이 있다/없다 if the action verb (동사) does not end in a final consonant.
    Use ~(으)ㄴ 적이 있다 to talk about things you have experienced in the past.
    Use ~(으)ㄴ 적이 없다 to talk about things you haven't experienced in the past.

자전거를 탄 적이 있어요?	Have you ever ridden a bicycle?
한국에 산 적이 없어요.	I have never lived in Korea.
만약에 그 것을 해 본 적이 없으면 조심하세요.	If you've never done this before, please be careful.
김치를 먹어 본 적이 있어요?	Have you ever eaten kimchi?
네, 먹어 본 적이 있는데 매웠어요.	Yes I have tried it, but it was spicy.

1A 경험

헌혈해 본 적이 있어요?
Have you ever tried donating blood?

총을 쏴 본 적이 있어요?
Have you ever tried shooting a gun?

명상을 해 본 적이 있나요?
Have you ever tried meditation?

헌혈 a blood drive | 혈액형 blood type | 사격장 a gun range | (총으로) 표적을 겨누다 to take aim at a target (with a gun) | 마음을 새롭게 하다 to freshen your mind | 평화를 찾다 to find peace | 중심을 잡다 to keep one's balance | 스트레스를 풀다 to relieve stress |

경험 ●1A

눈사람을 만들어 본 적이 있어요?
Have you ever made a snowman?

펜팔을 해 본 적이 있어요?
Have you ever tried having a pen-pal?

집 또는 공방에서 가구나 집에 쓸 물건을 직접 만들어 본 적이 있나요?
Have you ever built a household item at your house or in a workshop?

눈을 굴려 눈사람을 만들다 to roll the snow into a snowman | 언어 교환 language exchange | 주택개조 home improvement | (특히) 손으로 만들다 to craft | 손재주가 있다 to be good with your hands |

1A 경험

왕따를 당해 본 적이 있나요?
Have you ever been bullied?

몸싸움을 해 본 적이 있어요?
Have you ever been in a physical fight?

별명을 부르다 to be called names | 사이버 왕따 cyber-bullying | 손으로 치다 to punch |
뺨을 때리다 to slap | 발로 차다 to kick | 밀다 to push | 따돌림 당하다 to be ostracized |
눈에 멍이 들다 to have/get a black eye | 머리카락을 잡아당기다 to pull sbdy's hair |

경험 1A

할로윈데이에 사탕이나 초콜릿을 받으러 다닌 적이 있나요?
Have you ever gone trick-or-treating?

귀신이 나온다는 곳에 가 본 적이 있나요? 있다면 그 곳이 어디였나요?
Have you ever been somewhere haunted? If so, where was it?

코스튬을 입다 to wear a costume | 문을 두드리다 to knock on a door | 회의론자 a skeptic | 귀신 나오는 집 / 흉가 a haunted house | 폐가 an abandoned house

1A 경험

부모님 몰래 집을 빠져나간 적이 있나요? 어디에 다녀왔나요?
Have you ever snuck out without your parents knowing? Where did you go?

어디론가 몰래 숨어 들어가 본 적이 있나요? 있다면 어디인가요?
Have you ever snuck in somewhere you shouldn't have been? If so, where?

살금살금 가다 to go stealthily | 까치발로 걷다 to walk on tip-toe | 슬금슬금 달아나다 to sneak off

경험 1A

공적인 자리에서 옷 때문에 당황했던 적이 있나요? 지퍼가 고장나거나 옷이 흘러내렸던 경험이 있으면 이야기 해보세요. Have you ever had a wardrobe malfunction? If so, what happened?

도박을 해 본 적이 있나요?
Have you ever gone gambling?

지퍼를 잠그다 to have a zipper break | 바지가 찢어지다 to have your pants rip |
구두가 망가지다 to have your shoes break | 옷에 (물)을 쏟다 to spill (water) on your clothes |
돈을 걸다 to bet money | 돈을 따다 to win woney | 돈을 잃다 to lose money |

1A 경험

장난전화를 해 본 적이 있나요? 장난전화를 받은 적이 있나요?
Have you ever prank called someone? Has someone ever prank called you?

나이를 속인 적이 있나요?
Have you ever lied about your age?

~에게 장난을 치다 to play a joke on | 가짜 신분증 a fake ID | 미성년자 a minor (underage person) | 나이가 많은 척 하다 to pretend to be older | 어린 척 하다 to pretend to be younger |

경험 1A

대회에서 우승한 적이 있나요?
Have you ever won a contest?

기절한 적이 있어요? 있다면 무슨 일이 였나요?
Have you ever passed out? If so, what happened?

상금을 타다 to win a prize | 깨어나다 to wake up (after passing out) | 일등하다 to get first place | 꼴등하다 to get last place | 쓰러지다 to fall over | 어지럽다 to feel dizzy | 필름이 끊기다 to black out | 탈수증상 dehydration | 깨어나다 to wake | 더위를 먹다 (informal) to get heatstroke

1A 경험

이글루를 만들어 본 적이 있어요?
Have you ever tried making an igloo?

실수로 다른 사람에게 문자를 보낸 적이 있나요?
Have you ever sent a text to the wrong person by mistake?

누군가가 당신을 다른 사람이라고 착각하고 다가와 말을 한 적이 있나요?
Has anyone ever approached you thinking you were somebody else?

어색하다 to be awkward | 민망하다 to be embarrassing | 도플갱어 doppelganger | 닮다 to resemble |

경험 1A

케이블카를 타 본 적이 있어요?
Have you ever ridden a cable car?

....
....
....
....
....

어른들을 위한 색칠공부를 해 본 적이 있나요?
Have you ever done an adult coloring book?

....
....
....
....
....

장을 보러 시장에 가는 편인가요? 시장에 가면 그곳에서 주로 어떤 물건을 사나요?
Do you buy groceries at the market? If so, what do you usually buy there?

....
....
....
....
....
....
....

경치 scenery | 야경 night view | 고소공포증이 있다 to be afraid of heights | 생고기 fresh meat | 앞뒤로 흔들리다 to swing back and forth | 신선하다 to be fresh | 수제품 hand-made items | 벼룩시장 flea market | 야시장 night market |

1A 경험

스노우볼 효과를 경험한 적이 있나요? 어떤 일이 였는지 적어보세요.
Have you ever had something snowball out of control? If so, what?

공공장소에서 출입이 금지된 적이 있나요?
Have you ever been banned from a public place?

통제력을 벗어나다 to be out of one's control | 부담이 되다 to be a burden | 쫓겨나다 to be thrown out | 문제를 일으키다 to cause trouble | 말썽꾸러기 a troublemaker |

31

경험　1A

물건을 도둑 맞아 본 적이 있어요?
Have you ever had something stolen?

설명할 수 없을만큼 이상하거나 무서웠던 경험이 있나요?
Have you ever had a strange or scary encounter you can't explain?

집에 침입하다　a break-in　|　으스스하다　to be eerie / spooky　|　외계인을 보다　to see an alien　|　귀신을 보다　to see a ghost　|

1A 경험

잠결에 걸어 다녀 본 적이 있어요?
Have you ever sleepwalked?

옷의 무늬를 직접 염색 해 본 적이 있나요?
Have you ever tie-dyed your own clothes?

배심원의 한 사람으로 일해 본 적이 있나요?
Have you ever served on a jury?

스스로 하다 to do it yourself | 유죄를 선고하다 to convict sbdy | 무죄를 선고하다 to acquit sbdy | 재판 a court trial |

경험 ⬤ 1A

뭔가를 허위로 꾸며낸 적이 있나요? 그렇다면 무엇인가요?
Have you ever faked your way through something? If so, what?

다른 사람에 대한 소문을 퍼뜨린 적이 있나요? 있으면 누구였어요?
Have you ever started a rumour about somebody? If so about whom?

직접 손으로 다른사람에게 줄 선물을 만들어 본 적이 있나요? 있다면 무엇을 만들어 보았나요?
Have you ever made a gift for somebody else? If so, what?

가면 증후군 imposter syndrome | 감추다, 숨기다 to hide, conceal | 들키다 to be caught, found out | 소문이 나다 to have a rumor come out | 소문이 내다 to start a rumor | 소문이 퍼지다 to have a rumor spread |

1A 경험

가족중의 누군가 군대에 다녀온 적이 있나요?
Has a member of your family ever done military service?

군대에 입대해 본 적이 있나요? 있다면 그 경험은 어땠나요?
Have you ever done military service? If so, what was your experience like?

나라에 주둔하다 to be stationed in a country | 공군 airforce | 해군 navy | 군사 military | 제대하다 to be discharged from the army |

경험 1A

YouTube에 동영상을 올린 적이 있나요?
Have you ever uploaded a video to Youtube?

누군가의 뺨을 때린 적이 있나요?
Have you ever slapped someone?

이성을 잃고 다툰 적이 있나요? 만약 그렇다면 어떻게 그런 일이 일어났나요?
Have you ever lost your mind arguing with somebody? If so, how?

촬영하다 to film | 편집하다 to edit | 혼내다 to get mad at |

1A 경험

병원에 입원한 적이 있나요?
Have you ever been admitted to the hospital?

뼈가 부러진 적이 있나요? 있다면 어떻게 되었어요?
Have you ever broken a bone? If so, how?

입원하다 to be admitted to the hospital | 퇴원하다 to be discharged from the hospital |
엑스레이를 찍다 to get an x-ray | 깁스를 하다 to get a cast | 깁스를 떼다 to take off a cast |

경험 1A

실수로 누군가를 다치게 한 적이 있나요?
Have you ever accidentally injured someone?

감당하기 어려웠던 질병을 진단 받은 적이 있었나요?
Have you ever been diagnosed with something that was difficult to handle?

죄책감을 느끼다 to feel guilty | 당하다 to suffer/undergo sth | 참다 to endure | 힘이 세다 to be strong | 극복하다 to overcome |

1A 경험

이빨 교정을 해 본 적이 있나요?
Have you ever had braces?

왁싱을 해 본 적이 있나요?
Have you ever had anything waxed?

만약 성형 수술을 한다면 어떤 부분을 하고 싶나요?
If you were to have plastic surgery, what procedure would you opt for?

이가 비뚤다 to have crooked teeth | 이가 고르다 to have straight teeth | 화끈거리다 to feel a burning feeling on your skin | 따갑다 to feel a stinging feeling on your skin | 코수술 a nose job | 보톡스를 맞다 to get botox | 지방 흡입술 liposuction |

경험 — 1A

스키를 타 본 적이 있나요?
Have you ever gone skiing?

오토바이를 탄 적이 있나요? 없다면 오토바이를 타 보고 싶나요?
Have you ever ridden on a motorcycle? If not, would you want to?

크로스컨트리 cross-country skiing | 스키장 ski slope | 넘어지다 to fall over | 스키 점프 ski jump | 스노보드 snowboard | 위험하다 to be dangerous | 바람을 느끼다 to feel the wind | 신나다 to be exhilarating |

1A 경험

배를 타 본 적이 있나요?
Have you ever ridden on a boat?

LISTEN TO NATIVE SPEAKERS!

Video: 크루즈 여행 두번 해보고 느낀 솔직 장단점 A to Z
We went on two cruises: our honest thoughts on the advantages and disadvantages from A to Z

Channel: 잼쏭부부 jemissong

Level: 중급 (Intermediate)

예약하다 to book, to reserve | 일정을 짜다 to make a schedule | 장점 advantage |
단점 disadvantage | 파도가 세다 to have strong waves | 멀미 motion sickness |
해협 a straight/channel | 망망대해 the open sea | 햇살 sunshine | 선내 on-board |

경험 1A

스쿠버다이빙을 해 본 적이 있나요?
Have you ever been scuba diving?

카누나 카약을 타 본 적이 있나요?
Have you ever been canoing or kayaking?

흉터가 있나요? 있다면 어떻게 생겼어요?
Do you have a scar? If so, how did you get it?

스쿠버 다이빙 자격증 scubadiving certification | 잠수복 scubadiving suit | 산호초 coral reef | 바다 생물 sea creatures | (배가) 뒤집히다 (a boat) capsizes | 여울목 (river) rapids | 폭포 a waterfall | (배를) 젓다 to paddle (a boat) | 치유되다 sth heals | 흉터를 남기다 to leave a scar

1A 경험

자아를 찾고 싶었던 적이 있나요? 여전히 그것을 찾고 있나요?
Have you ever needed to find yourself? If so, are you still looking?

변화를 겪어본 적이 있어요? 만약 그렇다면, 무슨 일이 일어났었나요?
Have you ever gone through a transformation? If so, what did it involve?

방황하다 to feel lost | 사고뭉치 a trainwreck / a walking disaster | 신체적변화가 있다 to have a physical transformation | 더 성숙해지다 to become more mature | 라이프스타일이 변하다 to transform your lifestyle |

경험 　1A

누군가의 목숨을 살려 본 적이 있나요? 아니면 누군가가 당신의 생명을 구해 준 적이 있나요?
Have you ever saved anyone's life, or has anyone ever saved yours?

누군가를 바꾸려고 한 적이 있나요? 그 사람의 라이프 스타일이나 성격등과 같은 부분 말이예요.
Have you ever tried to change somebody? For example their lifestyle or personality.

죽을 고비를 넘기다　to have a near-death experience　|　영웅　hero　|　구세주　a savior　|
영향을 주다/미치다　to influence sbdy　|　나쁜 특성　a bad trait　|

1A 경험

신용카드 한도를 초과해 본 적이 있나요?
Have you ever maxed out your credit cards?

차에 기름이 떨어진 적이 있나요?
Has your car ever run out of gas?

밤을 새워 본 적이 있나요?
Have you ever stayed awake for an entire 24 hours?

카드 승인이 거절되다 to have your card declined | 파산하다 to be bankrupt | 견인하다 to tow | 갓길에 차를 세우다 to pull over to the shoulder | 파자마 파티 a sleepover | 밤샘 공부하다 to pull an all nighter |

경험 1A

경찰한테 잡혀 본 적이 있나요?
Have you ever been pulled over by a cop?

범죄현장의 목격자가 되어 증언 한 적이 있나요?
Have you ever witnessed a crime in progress?

속도위반 딱지를 받다 to get a speeding ticket | 빨간 불에 지나가다 to run a red light |
음주운전을 하다 to drink and drive | 범죄를 신고하다 to report a crime |

1A 경험

양궁을 해 본 적 있나요?
Have you ever tried archery?

깜짝파티를 해 본 적이 있나요?
Have you ever had a surprise party?

클럽에 가 본 적이 있나요?
Have you ever been clubbing?

활로 화살을 한 대 쏘다 to shoot an arrow with a bow | 과녁을 맞다 to hit the target | 과녁을 빗맞다 to miss the target | 과녁 한가운데에 적중하다 to get a bullseye | 밖순이 a party person | 하룻밤을 보내다 to have a one-night stand |

경험 1A

수술을 받아 본 적이 있어요? 있다면 어떤 수술을 받았어요?
Have you ever had surgery? If so, what was it for?

만약 내일 문신을 새겨야 한다면 어떤 문신을 새길건가요?
If you had to get a tattoo tomorrow, what would it be?

장학금을 받아 본 적이 있어요?
Have you ever won any scholarships?

마취하다 to anesthetize, to put sbdy under | 금식하다 to fast | 타투이스트 a tattoo artist | 전통적인 문신 a traditional tattoo | 수채화 문신 a watercolour tattoo | 문신 가게 a tattoo parlor | 성적 장학금 an academic scholarship | 체육 장학금 a sports scholarship |

1A 경험

부모님께 당신이 후회할만한 말을 한 적이 있나요?
Have you ever done something or said something to your parents that you regretted?

자동차 사고가 난 적이 있어요? 있다면 어떻게 되었던 일인지 설명 해 줄 수 있나요?
Have you ever been in a car accident? If so, what happened?

논쟁하다 to have an argument | 소리지르다 to shout | 뛰쳐나가다 to storm out | 감정을 상하게 하다 to hurt sbdy's feelings | 보험 정보를 교환하다 to exchange insurance information | 목이 뻐근하다 to get whiplash |

경험 　1A

SNS를 잠시쉬었던 적이 있어요? 없었다면 언제 SNS를 그만하고 싶다고 생각해요?
Have you ever taken a break from social media? Would you want to?

LISTEN TO NATIVE SPEAKERS!

Video: SNS를 끊고 생긴 4가지 변화
Four changes that happened when I quit social media

Channel: 더 나은 하루
Level: 고급 (Advanced)

SNS 중독　a social media addict　|　정신 건강　mental health　|　앱을 삭제하다　to delete an app　|
접다　to put aside　|　무의미하다　to be meaningless　|
너무 많은 인원들이 나의 관계 울타리망 속에 있다　to have too many people in your social life　|

1A 경험

룸메이트와 같이 산 적이 있나요? 제일 좋았거나 제일 별로였던 룸메이트 경험에 대해 설명하세요.
Have you ever had a roommate? Describe your best or worst roommate experience.

함께 나누다 to share | 자취 living alone |

1B 경험에 대한 원어민 답변예시

NATIVE KOREAN WRITING SAMPLES

1B 경험

1.1 대회에서 우승한 적이 있나요?
Have you ever won a contest?

어렸을때, 유치원에서 롯데가 주관하는 그림그리기 대회에 참여했던 적이 있는데, 어떤 건물의 모퉁이 부분만 그리려다 그마저도 다 못그려 전혀 기대하지 않고 있었는데 그림이 창의적이라며 2등으로 수상했던 기억이 있습니다. 그때, 엄청나게 큰 곰돌이 인형도 받았던 걸로 기억합니다.

1.2 대회에서 우승한 적이 있나요?
Have you ever won a contest?

네! 학교 철학 글쓰기 대회에서 금상을 탔어요. 저는 제가 금상을 탈 거라고는 생각하지도 못했는데 시상자 명단에 제가 있어서 깜짝 놀랐어요! 그때의 철학 글쓰기 주제는 '국가의 의무'였던 것 같아요. 어려운 주제여서 좋은 결과는 기대하지도 않았는데 뜻밖에 상을타게 돼서 너무 기뻤어요.

1.3 대회에서 우승한 적이 있나요?
Have you ever won a contest?

대회에 많이 나가보지 않았지만 고등학교때 정치관련 글쓰기에서 최우수상을 받은 적이 있어요. 그때가 박근혜가 대통령이었을 때인데, 현 정부의 문제점과 시행될 예정인 정책에 대해서 거의 3,000자 가까이 신랄한 비판을 했었죠.

경험　1B

1.4 대회에서 우승한 적이 있나요?
Have you ever won a contest?

나는 어렸을 때 피아노를 쳤었어. 피아노 학원을 다니면서 같이 배우는 친구들과 함께 지역 또는 국내 대회에 나가서 상을 받은 적이 있었지. 한 곡에 많은 시간과 노력을 들여서 짧은 순간에 평가 받는 일은 쉽지 않은 일이야. 자기 순서를 기다리는 것도 스트레스 받지. 하지만 친구들과 함께 경연에 나가서 내 차례를 기다리면서 마인드 컨트롤 할 수 있었어. 나를 도와 준 선생님과 친구들에게 감사해.

1.5 대회에서 우승한 적이 있나요?
Have you ever won a contest?

네. 작년 가을이었어요. 경상북도교육청에서 청소년 해커톤 대회(정식 명칭은 기억이 안나네요)를 했는데, 서너명씩 팀을 꾸려서 이틀 안에 프로그램을 하나 만들어내서 발표하는 대회였어요. 예선에 약 35팀이 참가했고 7팀이 본선에 진출했죠. 그리고 프로그램을 만들어서 (저희 팀이 만든 프로그램은 자습을 도와주는 프로그램이었어요) 발표했어요. 30분인가 1시간인가 후에 결과를 발표했는데 거기서 저희 팀이 1등이었어요.

1B 경험

1.6 대회에서 우승한 적이 있나요?
Have you ever won a contest?

초등학생때 영어 연극 대회를 나가서 우승한 적이 있어요. 친구들과 함께 미녀와 야수를 연극 했고 저는 야수에게 마법을 거는 요정 역할을 했어요. 제가 맡은 대사가 많지 않았지만 영어로 된 대사라서 부담을 느꼈어요. 그래서 대사를 수십번 암기했고 거울을 보며 연습했어요. 그리고 방과후에 친구들과 모여서 다함께 맞춰보았어요. 마침내 대회 날이 되었고 저는 실수 없이 제가 맡은 배역을 잘 해냈어요. 사회자 분께서 우리팀을 1등으로 호명했을 때 너무 기뻐서 다함께 소리지르며 환호했어요. 정말 보람차고 기쁜 순간이었어요.

경험　1B

2.1 귀신이 나온다는 곳에 가 본 적이 있나요? 있다면 그곳이 어디였나요?
Have you ever been somewhere haunted? If so, where was it?

네, 1995년 삼풍백화점 붕괴현장이었던 지금의 아크로비스타에서 밤에 지하층을 지나가다 멀리 흰 옷(자세히 기억은 안납니다.)입은 사람형태의 무언가를 보았습니다. 5분 뒤 다시 돌아왔을땐 없었습니다.

2.2 귀신이 나온다는 곳에 가 본 적이 있나요? 있다면 그곳이 어디였나요?
Have you ever been somewhere haunted? If so, where was it?

아무래도 1950년 일어난 한국 전쟁 때문에 전투가 일어난 곳을 밤에 가면 북한 인민군이나 중국 인민군의 귀신이 나오기도 합니다. 물론 한국군이나 UN연합군 귀신도 나온다는 지역도 있다고는 합니다.

2.3 귀신이 나온다는 곳에 가 본 적이 있나요? 있다면 그곳이 어디였나요?
Have you ever been somewhere haunted? If so, where was it?

귀신이 나온다는 곳에 가본 적은 없고 어렸을 때 놀이공원에서 귀신의 집이라는 공간에 가 본 적은 있어요. 진짜 귀신이 아니라 사람들이 만들어놓은 가짜 귀신이라고 알고 있었기 때문에 무섭지는 않았지만 어두운 공간에서 갑자기 귀신이 튀어나와서 깜짝 놀래키는 했었어요.

1B 경험

2.4 귀신이 나온다는 곳에 가 본 적이 있나요? 있다면 그곳이 어디였나요?
Have you ever been somewhere haunted? If so, where was it?

귀신이 나와서 가본 곳은 없지만 가서 보니까 귀신이 들렸던 것 같은 곳은 있어요. 몇년 전, 남자친구가 부모님과 함께 살 적에 그 집으로 놀러간 적이 있는데 남자친구의 방은 지하실에 있었어요. 한창 그 방에서 재밌게 놀다가 영화를 보게 됐는데 그 TV 위 장식장에 있던 뉴턴의 요람이 갑자기 혼자서 움직이더니 에너지 보존법칙에 의한 진자운동을 하기 시작했어요. 이렇게 말하니까 웃기긴한데 그 날 이후로 가끔가다가 전시해놓은 장난감들이 혼자서 움직인다던지 장식장에서 떨어진다던지 해서 소름이 돋았던 기억이 있네요.

2.5 귀신이 나온다는 곳에 가 본 적이 있나요? 있다면 그곳이 어디였나요?
Have you ever been somewhere haunted? If so, where was it?

귀신이 나온다는 곳이라.. 가본적 없네요 ㅋㅋㅋ

음 그래도 가끔 새벽에 집 들어갈 때 아파트 엘리베이터 타기가 좀 무서웠어요. 당연히 불도 켜져있고, 대단지 아파트라 건물도 많고 사는 사람도 많다보니 무슨 일이 일어나면 다들 나와서 확인하실테니 그다지 무서울건 없을 거라고 생각하실 수 있지만.. 괜히.. ㅎㅎ 무서운거 있잖아요? ㅋㅋㅋㅋ 그렇습니당~

경험 1B

2.6 귀신이 나온다는 곳에 가 본 적이 있나요? 있다면 그곳이 어디였나요? Have you ever been somewhere haunted? [...]

넵! 저는 겁이 많지는 않은 편이라ㅎㅎ 폐가체험을 해본적이 있는데, 귀신을 안믿으니 무섭진 않았지만 특유의 분위기가 귀신 무서워 하는 사람들에겐 정말 싫은 곳이었을거 같더라구요.

2.7 귀신이 나온다는 곳에 가 본 적이 있나요? 있다면 그곳이 어디였나요? Have you ever been somewhere haunted? [...]

가본적 없습니다. 근데 제가 생활하던 부대 막사에서 귀신이 나온다고 했어서 같이 살았던것 같네요.

2.8 귀신이 나온다는 곳에 가 본 적이 있나요? 있다면 그곳이 어디였나요? Have you ever been somewhere haunted? [...]

저는 귀신과 무당 같은 걸 믿는 편이라, 혹시라도 안 좋은 일이 생길까봐 절대로 일부러 그런 곳에 가지 않아요

2.9 귀신이 나온다는 곳에 가 본 적이 있나요? 있다면 그곳이 어디였나요? Have you ever been somewhere haunted? [...]

저는 공포 영화 같은 걸 보면 한 동안 트라우마에 시달리는 편이라 아예 보질 않아요. 귀신 나온다는 곳에 대해서 호기심은 엄청 가지만 아예 그런 정보는 차단하는 편입니다.

1B 경험

3.1 장을 보러 시장에 가는 편인가요? 시장에 가면 그곳에서 주로 어떤 물건을 사나요? Do you buy groceries at the market? [...]

시장은 잘 가지 않아요. 하지만 시장에서 꼭 사는 음식이 있다면 그건 떡일거예요. 특히 쑥떡이요. 큰 시장일수록 그리고 큰 떡집일수록 종류가 많고 맛있는 떡이 많답니다. 꼭 먹어보세요~

3.2 장을 보러 시장에 가는 편인가요? 시장에 가면 그곳에서 주로 어떤 물건을 사나요? Do you buy groceries at the market? [...]

저는 주로 코스트코를 갑니다. 주로 그 주에 필요한 품목 리스트를 만들어서 쇼핑을 시작하곤 하지만 결국 먹거나 쓰지도 않을 물건들을 충동적으로 구매해오곤 한답니다!

3.3 장을 보러 시장에 가는 편인가요? 시장에 가면 그곳에서 주로 어떤 물건을 사나요? Do you buy groceries at the market? If so, what do you usually buy there?

저는 장을 보러 대형마트에 주로 가요. 예전에 엄마를 따라 시장에 간적이 있어요. 저희 엄마는 여전히 시장에서 장을 보세요. 엄마는 할머니들이 손수 키우신 채소나 산에서 채집한 나물을 사요. 또 조개와 생선같은 해산물이나 방앗간에서 만든 떡과 밀가루도 시장에서 주로 사세요. 시장에 가면 먹을 거리도 많아요. 시장에는 싸고 맛있는 음식이 많아요. 엄마와 함께 장을 보고 나서 국수나 수제비를 사먹곤 했어요. 저에게 시장은 엄마와의 추억을 떠올리게 하는 곳이에요.

경험 1B

3.4 장을 보러 시장에 가는 편인가요? 시장에 가면 그곳에서 주로 어떤 물건을 사나요?
Do you buy groceries at the market? If so, what do you usually buy there?

저는 원래 시장에 가는 것을 좋아하는 편입니다. 상인들의 목소리와 시장 특유의 분위기가 살아있다는 느낌을 줍니다. 그래서 어렸을 때는 뭔가 스트레스를 받거나 심심할 때 동네에 시장 한 바퀴를 돌고는 했습니다. 그런데 최근에 이사를 하는 바람에 가까이에 시장이 없어서 마트만 이용하고 있어요 ㅠㅠ

3.5 장을 보러 시장에 가는 편인가요? 시장에 가면 그곳에서 주로 어떤 물건을 사나요?
Do you buy groceries at the market? If so, what do you usually buy there?

저는 시골에 살아서 시골 장이 열릴 때나 동네 작은 마트에 갑니다. 시골 장은 5일장이라고 해서 5일 마다 열리는 시장으로 저의 동네는 2일, 7일 로 끝나는 날마다 장이 열립니다. 장에 가면 일반 가게 보다 더 싸고 신선하게 살수 있고 노점상들도 와서 간식을 사기에도 좋습니다.

3.6 장을 보러 시장에 가는 편인가요? 시장에 가면 그곳에서 주로 어떤 물건을 사나요?
Do you buy groceries at the market? If so, what do you usually buy there?

아니요, 잘 안 가요. 제가 사는 동네는 계획에 따라 만들어진 신도시여서 시장이 없거든요. 가끔 명절이 되면 할머니 댁에 가는데, 그때는 시장에 가요! 제사를 준비하기 위해 식재료가 필요하거든요. 할머니 댁 주변 시장에서 과일, 생선, 떡 같은 먹을거리를 사요.

1B 경험

3.7 장을 보러 시장에 가는 편인가요? 시장에 가면 그곳에서 주로 어떤 물건을 사나요?
Do you buy groceries at the market? If so, what do you usually buy there?

시장은 주로 수산물시장을 자주 가는 편입니다. 저는 인천에 살아서 소래포구나 연안부두 같이 큰 수산물시장이 있어요. 특별한 날이 있을 때도 수산물시장을 가거나 아니면 특별한 저녁식사를 하고 싶을 때 수산물시장에 가서 그 날 싱싱한 해산물을 사고는 합니다. 서해 바다는 특히 꽃게가 유명하기 때문에 봄철이 되면 알이 밴 꽃게를① 사서 간장게장이나 양념게장을 해먹고 가을철이 되면 살이 통통하게 오른 숫꽃게를② 사서 꽃게찜을 해먹습니다.

¹ 꽃게: blue crab
² 숫꽃게: male blue crab (the females are called 암꽃게)

경험 1B

4.01 군대에 입대해 본 적이 있나요? 있다면 그 경험은 어땠나요? Have you ever done military service?

네, 군대는 해군에서 28개월 복무했고 군대경험은 될 수 있음 기억하고 싶지 않았다 정도로 정리하면 좋을 것 같네요.

4.02 군대에 입대해 본 적이 있나요? 있다면 그 경험은 어땠나요? Have you ever done military service?

네. 매우 좋지 않습니다. 자유를 빼앗긴 기분을 만끽할 수 있었습니다. 다시는 가고 싶지 않습니다.

4.03 군대에 입대해 본 적이 있나요? 있다면 그 경험은 어땠나요? Have you ever done military service?

네 국방의 의무를 다하였습니다. 그 경험에 대해 구술하라면 일주일을 떠들어도 모자라지만 한문장으로 요약한다면, 그 경험은 매우 좆같았습니다.

4.04 군대에 입대해 본 적이 있나요? 있다면 그 경험은 어땠나요? Have you ever done military service?

대한민국의 신체 건강한 남성이라면 모두 경험했을 것입니다 징병제 이니까요 그리고 입대할때의 느낌은 죽을맛 이었지만 제대하고 나서는 자기 만족감 이라고 할까 한동안은 마초맨으로 산것 같아요 ㅎㅎㅎ

1B 경험

4.05 군대에 입대해 본 적이 있나요? 있다면 그 경험은 어땠나요? Have you ever done military service?

군대에 입대한 적이 없어요. 한국에서는 남자들만 병역의무가 있고 여자는 의무는 없고 희망자에 한해서만 직업군인이 되는 형식이기 때문에 여자인 저는 군대에 가본 적이 없어요.

4.06 군대에 입대해 본 적이 있나요? 있다면 그 경험은 어땠나요? Have you ever done military service?

저는 내년 말 즈음에 입대할 예정입니다. 제 또래 친구들은 이미 입대해서 군 생활을 하고 있답니다. 슬픔니다. 책이 나올 때면 저는 군대에서 행군을 하고 있지 않을까요? ㅋㅋ

4.07 군대에 입대해 본 적이 있나요? 있다면 그 경험은 어땠나요?
Have you ever done military service? If so, what was your experience like?

아직 군대에 입대하지는 않았지만, 곧 해야 돼요. 우리나라는 징병제 국가여서 남자는 군대에 무조건 가야 되거든요. 군대에 가야한다는 생각 때문에 요즘 너무 스트레스 받아요. 한창 젊은 나이인 20대에 폐쇄적인 군대에 들어간다는 것 자체가 스트레스가 돼요. 거기다 우리나라 군대에서는 군인들에게 최저시급도 주지 않아요. 사람으로서 받아야 할 가장 최소한의 배려도 받지 못하는 곳이 군대인 것 같아요.

경험 1B

4.08 군대에 입대해 본 적이 있나요? 있다면 그 경험은 어땠나요?
Have you ever done military service? If so, what was your experience like?

여러 지역에서 여러 명이 오다보니 이런 사람 저런 사람이 있더라고요. 친하지는 않았어도 20년 넘은 지금도 이름이 기억날 정도로 인상적인 사람도 있어요. 사격이 제일 재밌었어요. 편한 부대였는데도 전역 후 15년 정도는 매년 다시 군대에 가는 악몽을 꿨는데, 지금은 워리어플랫폼[1] 사업이 진행 중이고, 그런 장비들을 만져보고 싶다는 생각을 한 이후로는 재입대 악몽을 꾸지않고 있습니다.

4.09 군대에 입대해 본 적이 있나요? 있다면 그 경험은 어땠나요?
Have you ever done military service? If so, what was your experience like?

넵! 한국남자라면 대부분 군대에 입대하게 되죠? 그중에서 저는 특별하게도 카투사라는 보직으로 입대를 하게 됐었어요. 카투사는 Korean Augmentation to the U.S. Army의 약어에요!! 미국도 못가본 제가 미군부대에서 생활해봤는데 정말 너무 좋았어요ㅠ 편하다면 편했지만 한국군의 거울이 될 수도 있다는 생각에 일하거나 훈련받을 땐 누구보다 열심히 했던 기억이 있네요. 군입대는 지금까지도 제일 인상깊은 추억 중 하나에요.

---

[1] 워리어플랫폼 (Warrior Platform) is an initiative to modernize military equipment in Korea, including combat uniforms, combat shoes, bulletproof suits, first aid kits, personal firearms, supplementary equipment, and night vision.

1B 경험

4.10 군대에 입대해 본 적이 있나요? 있다면 그 경험은 어땠나요?
Have you ever done military service? If so, what was your experience like?

전 군대에 입대해 본적은 없지만, 제 오빠는 2년동안 육군으로서 일했고 외삼촌은 해병대의 연대장으로서 이바지하셨어요. 오빠가 말한 바로는 좋은 경험이었지만 다시 돌아가기는 싫다고 했어요.

4.11 군대에 입대해 본 적이 있나요? 있다면 그 경험은 어땠나요?
Have you ever done military service? If so, what was your experience like?

네. 2019년 11월18일에 입대 했었고 2021년 6월3일에 전역했습니다. 저는 한국의 시베리아로 불리는 강원도 철원에서 군생활을 보냈습니다. 재밌었던 경험이라면 강원도는 눈이 많이와서 주말에 쉬어야하지만 눈이 너무 쌓여서 제설을 많이했던 기억이 있네요. 또 군대생활관 동기들과 저녁에 라면을 간부들 몰래 먹었었던 기억이있네요. 뿌듯했던 경험은 훈련 종료후에 내가 무언가를 해서 훈련이 성공적으로 마쳤던 기억입니다. 안좋은 기억도 있는데요. 군대에서 훈련을 하다가 간부의 실수로 제가 팔윗부분을 베이게 되었는데 흉터로 남았네요. 간부가 사과를 안해서 그다지 안좋은 기억으로 남았습니다. 종합적으로 군대에서의 경험이 어땠냐고 평을 내린다면 "그 때 동기들과 함께한다면 한 번은 다시 할 수 있다 입니다."

경험 1B

5.1 물건을 도둑 맞아 본 적이 있어요?
Have you ever had something stolen?

네. 어렸을 때 아파트 1층에 살았는데요. 엄마랑 동생이랑 외출을 하고 돌아오니까 집안이 난장판이 되어있더라구요. 도둑이 들었던거죠. 제가 태어날 때부터 어른들한테 받은 용돈을 모두 넣어논 엄청 큰 돼지 저금통을 도둑 맞았어요. 그거 풀었으면 한 100만원은 넘었을텐데……

5.2 물건을 도둑 맞아 본 적이 있어요?
Have you ever had something stolen?

어릴 때 비싼 게임기를 집에 놀러온 친구에게 보여줬다가 사라져서 엉엉 울었어요. 그러고 몇 주 뒤 친구가 돌려줬는데 아무리 봐도 산 게 아니라 제꺼였어요. 그 뒤론 그 친구랑은 말도 안했던 기억이 나요.

5.3 물건을 도둑 맞아 본 적이 있어요?
Have you ever had something stolen?

옛날에 초5(12살)때? 비 오는 날이었어요. 당시 제가 다니던 학원[1]은 학원 들어가는 문 바로 앞에 우산을 두게 되어 있었어요. 거기에 제가 쓰고 온 빨간 우산을 뒀었죠. 근데 끝나고 집에 가려니 그 우산이 사라졌어요. 그 후로 그 우산을 다시 보지 못했어요.

---

[1] 학원 (hagwon) is an after-school training academy specializing in extra curricular activities including additional schooling, musical instruments, and sports activities. Most Korean children attend at least one (often more) hagwons in addition to regular school.

1B 경험

5.4 물건을 도둑 맞아 본 적이 있어요?
Have you ever had something stolen?

음....딱 한번 있어요. 고등학생 시절인데, 제가 쓰는 샤프(mechanical pencil) 하나가 사라진 적이 있어요. 내가 잃어버린 건 아니고, 누가 훔쳤구나 생각하고 며칠간 학생들이 뭘 들고 다니는지 잘 관찰했었습니다. 3일 뒤 같은 반 학생이 자기 가방을 뒤적거리는데 거기서 제 샤프가 나오더군요. 보자마자 그거 내껀데 왜 너가 가지고 있냐 하니까 머쓱해 하더라구요. 불같이 화를 내고 다시 가져왔습니다.

5.5 물건을 도둑 맞아 본 적이 있어요?
Have you ever had something stolen?

물건을 도둑 맞아 본 적이 있습니다. 친구에게 생일 선물로 북한에서 공수된 담배 한 갑을 준 적이 있습니다. 어느 순간 그 담배가 보이지 않더라고요. 선물을 준 친구가 제 룸메이트였는데 북한 담배를 많이 핀 모습을 본 적이 없는데 어느 순간부터 보이지 않더라고요. 저희 모두 매우 의아해 했습니다. 하지만, 다른 친구네 집을 가보니 제가 룸메이트가 선물로 준 담배가 있더라고요. 정말 황당하고 얼척이① 없었죠.

---

[1] 얼척이 없다 - a Cheon-nam dialect for the idiom 어이가 없다 = "I'm speechless", "this makes no sense", or "this is ridiculous"; it has a slight "WTF?" feeling.

경험 　1B

5.6 물건을 도둑 맞아 본 적이 있어요?
Have you ever had something stolen?

비싼 물건은 아니지만, 작은 무선 스탠드를 학교에서 도둑맞은 적이 있어요. 제가 다니던 학교는 기숙사 학교인데 매일 저녁 11시까지 공부를 해야 했어요. 제가 공부하던 자리는 불이 어두워서 스탠드가 필요했죠. 그래서 집에서 조그만 스탠드를 가져가 공부를 하곤 했는데, 어느 날 그걸 도둑맞은 거 있죠? 정말 어이가 없었답니다.

5.7 물건을 도둑 맞아 본 적이 있어요?
Have you ever had something stolen?

도둑 맞은적은 없지만 눈뜨고 코베인[1] 경우는 있습니다. 10년도 더 지난 일이지만 아주 어릴적에 부모님께서 어린이 시계를 사준 적이 있었는데 같은 어린이집 다니는 친구가 자기도 한번만 차 보고싶다고 빌려가더니 그 다음날 제 시계를 자기네 부모님이 사준 시계고 자기것 이라며 저보고 남의 것 탐내지 말라고 하더군요. 이것도 도둑질의 일환으로 봐야하나요? 일단 살면서 물건을 뺏기거나 도둑맞았다고 말할만한게 이것 밖에 없네요. 이때 배신감에 크게 데여 본인 물건에 민감해진 영향도 있기에 그런 경험이 덜한 것도 있겠네요.

[1] 눈뜨고 코베인다 - [눈을 뜨고 코를 베인다] - an idiom meaning literally "blink your eyes, and you'll lose your nose". It's used in situations where sth bad happens to you, and you're surprised, but you really should have seen it coming. You feel dumb for not anticipating it.

1B 경험

NOTES

경험 1B

NOTES

1B 경험

NOTES

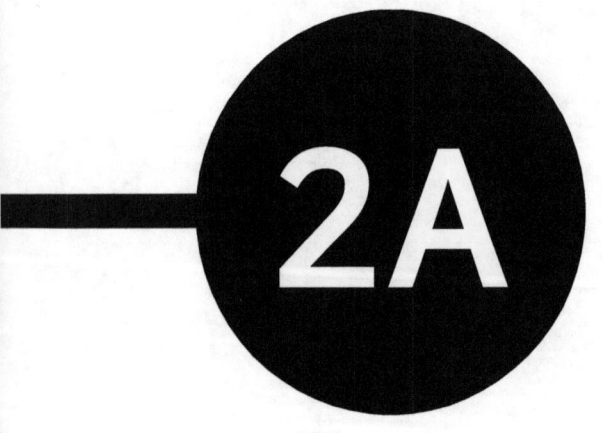

2A 능력에 대한 질문
QUESTIONS ABOUT ABILITIES

문법

~을/를 수 있다/없다

TO TALK ABOUT THINGS YOU CAN OR CAN'T DO

Video: [한국어 초급 문법] -(으)ㄹ 수있다 Korean basic grammar
저는 수영을 할 수 있어요
Channel: A Piece of Korean 한국어 한 조각
TOPIK: 1급 (초급)

WATCH A VIDEO LESSON!

This grammar form can be attached to action verbs (동사)
    Use ~을 수 있다/없다 if the action verb (동사) ends in a final consonant (받침)
    Use ~를 수 있다/없다 if the action verb (동사) does not end in a final consonant (받침)
    Use ~을/를 수 있다 to talk about actions you can do.
    Use ~을/를 수 없다 to talk about actions you can't do.
It is used to talk about abilities and possibilities.

피아노를 칠 수 있어요.	I can play the piano.
김치가 매워서 먹을 수 없어요.	Kimchi is spicy so I can't eat it.
이해할 수 없으면 말해 주세요.	If you can't understand please tell me.
중국어는 말할 수 없지만 한국어는 말할 수 있어요.	I can't speak Chinese but I can speak Korean.
작년에는 턱걸이를 전혀 할 수 없었어요.	I couldn't do a pull-up at all last year.

문법

~을/를 줄 알다/모르다

TO TALK ABOUT THINGS YOU KNOW OR DON'T KNOW HOW TO DO

WATCH A VIDEO LESSON!
Video: 한국어 배우기 | 한국어 문법 64: V-을/ㄹ 줄 알다[모르다] - Learn Korean | Basic Korean Grammar
Channel: 베이직 코리안 Basic Korean
TOPIK: 4급 (중급)

This grammar form can be attached to action verbs (동사)
 Use ~을 줄 알다/모르다 if the action verb (동사) ends in a final consonant (받침)
 Use ~를 줄 알다/모르다 if the action verb (동사) does not end in a final consonant(받침)
 Use ~을/를 줄 알다 to talk about an action you know how to do
 Use ~을/를 줄 모르다 to talk about an action you don't know how to do
It is used to talk about abilities and things you've learned.

한국어를 말할 줄 아세요?	Do you know how to speak Korean?
김치를 만들 줄 알아요?	Do you know how to make kimchi?
배운 적이 없어서 스키를 탈 줄 몰라요.	I don't know how to ski because I haven't learned.
한국어를 말하기는 잘 못하지만 한글은 읽을 줄 알아요.	I can't speak Korean very well, but I know how to read the alphabet.

2A 능력

요리를 잘 하세요?
Are you a good cook?

체스를 할 수 있나요?
Can you play chess?

당구를 칠 수 있나요?
Can you play pool?

루빅 큐브를 잘 하나요?
Can you solve a Rubik's Cube?

요리법 / 조리법 / 레시피 recipe | 요리책 a recipe book | 전략적이다 to be strategic | 당구채 a pool cue | 당구대 a pool table | 색깔을 맞추다 to match colors |

능력 2A

저글링을 할 수 있어요?
Can you juggle?

풍선껌을 불 수 있나요?
Can you blow a bubble with bubblegum?

외국어를 할 줄 아세요?
Can you speak a foreign language?

휘파람을 불 수 있나요?
Can you whistle?

손과 눈을 연결하는 조정력이 좋다 to have good hand-eye coordination | 모국어 native language | 공중으로 던지다 to throw in the air | 얼굴에 달라붙다 to stick to your face | 2개국어를 하다 to be bilingual | 휘파람으로 곡을 부른다 to whistle a tune |

2A 능력

바디랭귀지를 잘 이해 할 수 있어요?
Are you good at understanding body language?

노래 잘 부르세요?
Are you a good singer?

춤 잘 추세요?
Are you a good dancer?

눈치가 있다 to be aware of social cues | 무대 공포증 stage fright | 가창력 singing ability |
음치 sbdy who is tone deaf | 몸치 sbdy with two left feet | 박치 no sense of rhythm |
동작이 우아하다 to have graceful movements | 리듬감이 좋다 a good sense of rhythm |

능력 2A

성대모사를 잘 해요?
Are you good at impersonations?

텐트를 설치 할 수 있어요?
Can you set up a tent?

고장난 물건을 잘 고치는 편인가요?
Are you good at fixing things?

흉내내다 to imitate | 말투 an accent | 복잡하다 to be complex | 설명서 instruction guide | 해결하다 to solve |

2A 능력

현재 독학(스스로 공부하는것)하고 있거나 과거에 독학으로 배운 것이 있나요?
Are you "self-taught" in anything? Is there anything you're teaching yourself now?

기계를 잘 다루세요?
Are you good with electronics and machines?

동기 motivation | 열정 passion | 컴맹 sbdy who is computer illiterate | 기계치 sbdy who is technologically challenged | 마음먹다 to decide / to make up your mind | 실천하다 to put one's plan into action | 컴맹 sbdy who is computer illiterate |

능력

어떤 타고난 재능이 있나요?
What talent are you gifted at, that comes naturally?

악기를 연주할 수 있어요?
Can you play a musical instrument?

터득하다 to get the hang of sth / to have a knack for sth | 연주회   a recital / performance |
악보   sheet music |

2A 능력

왼손잡이 인가요? 오른손 잡이 인가요?
Are you left-handed or right-handed?

어떤 별자리를 알고 있나요?
Which constellations do you know?

젓가락을 사용할 수 있어요?
Can you use chopsticks?

넥타이를 맬 줄 알아요?
Can you tie a tie?

양손잡이다 to be ambidextrous | 별을 보다 to stargaze | 젓가락질이 서투르다 to be awkward with chopsticks | 집다 to pick up | 나무젓가락을 쪼개다 to break apart wooden chopsticks |

능력 2A

베이킹을 할 수 있어요?
Can you bake?

어떤 자격증을 가지고 있나요?
Do you have any special licenses or titles?

약속을 잘지키는 편인가요?
Do you tend to stick to your commitments?

팬에 붙다 to stick to the pan | (빵)이 잘 부풀다 the (bread) rises well | 클러치판 the clutch | 똑바로 되다 for sth to be done properly | 약속을 어기다 to break a promise | 거짓말하다 to lie

2A 능력

수동으로 운전을 할 줄 알아요?
Can you drive a stick-shift?

운전을 잘 하나요?
Are you a good driver?

자동차 an automatic car | 차가 멈추다 the car stalls | 시동이 걸리다 to restart (the car) | 기어를 바꾸다 to shift/change gears | 평행 주차 parallel parking | 서투르다 to be unskilled | 난폭운전 / 보복운전 road rage | 속도 제한 the speed limit |

능력 2A

사교적인 편이예요?
Do you have good social skills?

감정을 솔직하게 표현하는 편인가요?
Are you good at expressing how you feel?

대인관계 interpersonal relations | 사회 불안 social anxiety | 비사교적이다 to be unsociable |
활발하다 to be lively / animated | 꿔다 놓은 보릿자루 sbdy who is 'a stick in the mud' |
감정을 숨기다 to hide feelings | 인정하다 to recognize / acknowledge |

2A 능력

유머감각이 있어서 다른 사람들을 잘 웃기는 편인가요?
Are you good at making other people laugh?

비판을 잘 받아들이는 편인가요?
How well do you take criticism?

농담을 하다 to tell a joke | 유치하다 to be silly | 바보 같다 to be a fool | 엉뚱하다 to be over the top | 비판을 통해 배우다 to learn from criticism | 예민하다 to take things personally | 덤덤하다 to be thick-skinned | 비판을 무시하다 to ignore criticism |

능력　2A

옆돌기를 할 줄 알아요?
Can you do a cartwheel?

다리 찢기를 할 수 있어요?
Can you do the splits?

턱걸이를 할 수 있어요?
Can you do a pull-up?

1마일(2km)을 달리는 데 얼마나 걸리나요?
How long does it take you to run one mile?

균형감각이 좋다　to have a good sense of balance　|　균형을 잃다　to lose your balance　|
유연하다　to be flexible　|　스트레칭을 하다　to stretch　|　상체 힘　upper body strength　|
상체 운동　upper body exercizes　|　상태가 좋다　to be in good shape　|

2A 능력

철인 3종경기에 대해 들어봤어요? 있다면 참가해볼 생각이 있나요?
Have you heard of triathalons? Would you ever consider participating in one?

방향 감각이 좋은편이예요?
Do you have a good sense of direction?

길가에서 타이어가 터졌다면 도움없이 혼자 타이어를 교체 할 수 있나요?
If your car broke down on the road, could you change your tire without help?

훈련하다 to train | 일정을 지키다 to keep to a schedule | 인내심 endurance | 길치 sbdy with no sense of direction | 길을 잃다 to get lost | 어디에 있는지 기억을 잘하다 to remember where you've been | 자립적이다 to be self-reliant | 스페어 타이어 a spare tire |

능력 2A

돈을 잘 관리하는 편인가요?
How financially responsible are you?

LISTEN TO NATIVE SPEAKERS!

Video: **FLEX도 습관? 대학생의 통장 털기**
Treat yo' self? Raiding college students' bank statements

Channel: 이십세들 (Twenty Birds)
Level: 고급 (Advanced)

잔액 bank balance | 신용카드 a credit card | 소비습관 consumption habits | 충동적이다 to be impulsive | 돈을 모으다 to save money | 함부로 recklessly / carelessly | 계좌 bank account | 생활비 living costs | 용돈 pocket money | 월급 monthly salary |

2A 능력

공부를 잘하는 편이예요? 학창시절에 모범생이였나요?
Do you do well academically? Were you a model student during your school days?

다른 사람이랑 쉽게 친해지는 편인가요?
Is it easy for you to get along with people?

일반학생 an average student | 외향적이다 to be extroverted | 내성적이다 to be introverted | 좋은 성적 good grades | 학구적이다 to be academic | 잘 맞다 to match well | 상대 the other person | 헛똑똑이 sbdy who is only "book smart" | 말을 걸다 strike up a conversation |

2B 능력에 대한 원어민 답변예시
NATIVE KOREAN WRITING SAMPLES

2B 능력

6.1 기계를 잘 다루세요?
Are you good at handling electronics and machines?

아니요. 기계를 잘 못 다루고, 기계 관련 매뉴얼을 보는 것을 항상 귀찮아 해요.

6.2 기계를 잘 다루세요?
Are you good at handling electronics and machines?

기계에 따라 다르지만. 보통 여자들 보다는 기계 만지는거에 거부감이 없고. 어렸을 때 부터 이것 저것 혼자 손보기도 했어요.

6.3 기계를 잘 다루세요?
Are you good at handling electronics and machines?

기계다루기를 좋아합니다. 제가 가지고 있는 오토바이의 소모품은 거의 제가 집접 교체를 합니다. 엔진오일, 브레이크 라이닝, 타이어 등등

6.4 기계를 잘 다루세요?
Are you good at handling electronics and machines?

간단한 기계는 설명서 없이 사용 가능합니다. 복잡한 기계도 설명서만 있다면 가능하구요. 물론 원리적인 부분이나 수리같은 부분은 논외입니다.

능력 2B

6.5 기계를 잘 다루세요?
Are you good at handling electronics and machines?

잘 다루는 편이에요. 저는 언니가 있는데 언니는 기계치인것에 반해 저는 이것저것 잘 다루는 편이여서 항상 집에 무언가 고쳐야 하거나 기계에 관련된 일은 제가 했던 것 같아요.

6.6 기계를 잘 다루세요?
Are you good at handling electronics and machines?

네, 잘 다룹니다. 저는 어릴때부터 기계를 다루는 것을 좋아했어요. 그래서 지금은 왠만한 기계들은 고장이 나거나 작동에 오류가 있으면 직접 고치고 조립하는 것도 무리없이 해내는 편입니다.

6.7 기계를 잘 다루세요?
Are you good at handling electronics and machines?

모든 기계를 잘 다루진 않습니다. 다만 어느정도 실생활에 활용되는 것들은 최소한의 사용설명서가 있다면 잘 사용할 수 있습니다. 예를 들면 간단히 건전지를 갈거나, 조립을 하는 것 쯤은 할 수 있지만 고장난 것의 원인을 찾아 고치거나 처음 보는 기계는 잘 다루지 못합니다. 사실 유투브나 다양한 매체를 통해서 배울 수는 있지만 저의 경우는 새로운 기계를 다루고 배워야할 때는 반드시 사람을 만나서 직접 배워야 활용할 수 있습니다. 이렇게 이야기를 하고 있지만 전 사실 기계치라는 말을 많이 듣는 사람중에 한 명이랍니다.

2B 능력

6.8 기계를 잘 다루세요?
Are you good at handling electronics and machines?

저는 '기계치'에요. 어릴때 제 동생은 새로운 기기나 기계들을 잘 다루어서 지금은 삼성전자에 취직해서 근무 하고 있어요. 하지만 저는 그렇지 못해서 새로운 기기를 구입했을때 사용설명서를 참고해도 저에게는 내용이 복잡해서, 인터넷을 통해(유튜브 영상) 방법을 터득할 정도에요. 그래서, 기계를 잘 다루고, 응용할 줄 아는 사람들이 늘 부러워요.

능력 2B

7.1 외국어를 할 줄 아세요?
Can you speak another language?

외국어는 영어랑 일본어를 할 줄 알아요. 영어는 중학교부터 학교에서 배웠었고, 일본어는 제가 일본문화를 좋아해서 '독학'으로 배우고 있는 중이에요.

7.2 외국어를 할 줄 아세요?
Can you speak another language?

네 저는 영어를 할 수있어요. 제 생각에 대부분 한국인들은 영어를 외국어로 제일 잘 할 것 같아요. 왜냐하면 학창시절 내내 영어를 배우거든요. 안타까운 것은 수능을 위한 영어라 말하기보다는 그냥 테스트를 위한 영어를 배우지만요.

7.3 외국어를 할 줄 아세요?
Can you speak another language?

네, 영어를 할 수있어요. 일상적인 대화들은 무리없이 하는 편입니다. 하지만 상대방의 말하는 발음이나 속도로 인해서 잘 못알아 듣는경우도 있고 모르는 단어나 관용구를 사용할때도 이해하는데 어려움이 있기도 합니다. 그래서 영어는 계속 공부하고 있는 외국어입니다. 그리고 저는 일본어와 독일어를 공부한적이 있지만 간단한 표현 외에는 잘하지 못합니다.

2B 능력

7.4 외국어를 할 줄 아세요?
Can you speak another language?

영어랑 일본어 조금 할 줄 알아요. 그런데 제 생각에는 제가 외국어의 억양을 잘 따라하는 것 같아요. 그래서 몇 마디 할 줄 몰라도 그 약간으로 그 외국어를 엄청 잘하는 것 같은 오해를 불러일으키는 스타일인것 같아요. 제가 일본어는 제가 할 줄 아는 말만 할 수 있는 정도인데요. 일본에 가서 현지 분에게 어떤거 물어보거나 대답하면 제가 일본어 엄청 잘하는 줄 알고 대답을 정말 길게해주세요. 그런 전 "스.... 스미마셍......"[1] 이렇게 대답하죠.

7.5 외국어를 할 줄 아세요?
Can you speak another language?

고등학교때 일본어를 배웠고, 꽤 잘했는데 지금은 제 이름만 소개하는 정도만 말할 수 있어요. 현재 미국에 살고 있기 때문에 영어를 배우고 있고, 사용하고 있어요. 생각보다 언어를 배우는게 정말 어렵다는걸 몸소 체험하고 있는데요. 아이들을 키우고 일을 하다보니 언어를 배우는게 생각보다 어렵고 하는말만 하게 되는 경향이 있더라구요. 그래도 계속 살다보면 아주 조금씩이라도 더 좋아지지 않을까 하고 생각합니다.

---

[1] 스미마셍 is the Korean pronunciation for the Japanese word "sumimasen" which means something like "excuse me" or "I'm sorry."

능력 2B

8.1 다른 사람이랑 쉽게 친해지는 편인가요?
Is it easy for you to get along with people?

그런것 같기도 하고, 아닌것 같기도 하네요. 어른이 되고나서는 좀 편하게 친해지는 것 같기도해요.

8.2 다른 사람이랑 쉽게 친해지는 편인가요?
Is it easy for you to get along with people?

네, 그런 편인데요. 나이 들어가면서 새로운 사람과 친해지는 기회가 줄어들고 저도 새로운 만남을 굳이 시도하려고 하지 않아요.

8.3 다른 사람이랑 쉽게 친해지는 편인가요?
Is it easy for you to get along with people?

아닌것 같아요. 저는 친해지는데 시간이 걸리는 편인거 같아요. 처음 만난 사람과 가벼운 이야기는 할 수 있지만, 그렇게 편하지는 않는 것 같아요. 무슨 얘기를 해야 하는지도 어려운 것 같아요. 상대가 조금 저와 비슷하거나 잘 맞는 경우는 괜찮지만, 저랑 조금 다른 성향의 사람은 친해지기가 어려운 것 같아요. 어렸을때는 이런저런 생각없이 잘 친해졌던 것 같은데, 확실히 나이를 먹어가면서 사람을 사귀는게 어려워져 가는 것 같아요. 가끔은 그렇다는게 슬프기도 하지만, 한편으로는 자연스러운 일이라고 생각이 들어요.

2B 능력

8.4 다른 사람이랑 쉽게 친해지는 편인가요?
Is it easy for you to get along with people?

네. 쉽게 친해지는 편입니다. 제가 여러가지 취미활동을 하는데 특히 상대방이 같은 취미를 즐기면 더 많은 이야기를 하게되고 더쉽게 친해지는 것 같습니다. 저는 모터바이크, 카약, 당구, 수영, 골프, 낚시를 즐깁니다.

8.5 다른 사람이랑 쉽게 친해지는 편인가요?
Is it easy for you to get along with people?

네 금방 친해지는 편입니다. 제가 어색한 분위기를 못 견뎌하는 편이라서요. 제가 주도해서 먼저 말을 걸어요. 그런데 깊은 관계가 되기까지는 좀 오래 걸리는 것 같아요. 제가 사람을 잘 못 믿나봐요. 하하.

8.6 다른 사람이랑 쉽게 친해지는 편인가요?
Is it easy for you to get along with people?

네, 잘 친해지는 편이예요. 저는 주변의 친한 사람들의 연령대가 다양한 편입니다. 다른 사람들에게 쉽게 다가가는 편입니다. 하지만 아무나 친해지려고 하거나 먼저 나서서 친해지려고 하지는 않아요. 적어도 자연스러운 만남이나 직업적인 이유 혹은 필요에 따라서 다른 사람들과 친해지려고 할때는 어려움이 없이 다가갈 수 있어요.

능력 2B

8.7 다른 사람이랑 쉽게 친해지는 편인가요?
Is it easy for you to get along with people?

다른 사람이랑 쉽게 친해지는 편이에요. 개인적으로 대인관계에서 '예의'를 중요하게 여기는 편이라 상대의 말투나 표현, 행동등 '말의 품격'이 느껴지는 분들과는 더 쉽게 친해져요. 한국 속담중에 "말 한마디에 천냥 빚을 갚는다."의 문구에 많이 동감해요. 말은 그 사람의 사회적 배경과 성품을 들어낸다고 믿기에, 깍듯하고 예의를 갖춘 사람들과는 건강한 관계를 지속할 수 있는 것 같아요.

8.8 다른 사람이랑 쉽게 친해지는 편인가요?
Is it easy for you to get along with people?

친해진다는 것의 정도와 의미는 사람마다 다 다르겠지만 저는 처음 만나는 사람들과 좋은 관계를 맺고 친해지는 친화력은 있어요. 그래서 누군가를 만나면 쉽게 마음을 열고 친해집니다. 하지만 조금 더 깊은 관계가 되기 위해서는 시간이 필요한 편입니다. 그 사람에 대해서 알아가면서 나의 소신과 가치관이 다르면 더 깊은 관계로는 발전하진 못하지만 가볍게 이야기 하는 것은 불편하지 않는 것 같아요. 사실 나이를 먹으면서 진실한 친구를 만나고 얻어가는것이 쉽지는 않지만 저는 제가 먼저 마음을 잘 주기 때문에 제 입장에서는 쉽게 친해진다고 말할 수 있습니다. 뭐 상대방은 모르겠지만요. ㅋ

[1] "말 한마디에 천냥 빚을 갚는다" - literally means "you can pay back a debt of 1000 nyang (old Korean currency) with just a word" meaning "if you speak well, even difficult tasks become simple." It highlights how speaking kindly or charismatically can diffuse a bad situation.

2B 능력

9.1 약속을 잘지키는 편인가요?
Do you tend to stick to your commitments?

네 약속을 잘 지키는 편입니다. 특히 시간 약속에 좀 민감한 편이에요. 그래서 스트레스를 많이 받아요. 그런데 하나 잘 못지키는 약속이 있어요. 바로 자신과의 다이어트 약속이요.

9.2 약속을 잘지키는 편인가요?
Do you tend to stick to your commitments?

약속은 잘지키는편이예요. 늦는것을 별로 좋아하지 않아서 일찍일찍 나가지만..요새 시작한 운전이 서툴러서 제의도와 다르게 늦는것같아요ㅋ 그래도 늦을때면 먼저 문자나 전화로 늦는다고 연락을 하는편이예요.

9.3 약속을 잘지키는 편인가요?
Do you tend to stick to your commitments?

네, 잘지키는 편입니다. 중요한 약속은 반드시 지켜야 하는것은 당연하겠지요. 무엇보다 가족이나 가까운 친구들과 약속을 할 경우엔 보다 철저하게 지키려고 노력합니다. 왠지 약속을 잘 지키지 않는 사람은 신뢰가 가지 않는다는 인식때문인것 같아요. 그렇다고 제가 늘 완벽하게 약속을 지키는 사람은 아닙니다.

능력 2B

9.4 약속을 잘지키는 편인가요?
Do you tend to stick to your commitments?

잘 지키는 편인 것 같아요. 항상 늦지 않게 출발하거나, 일을 미리미리 준비하는 편인데 가끔 차가 막힌다거나, 아프다거나 하는 변수가 있긴 해요.

9.5 약속을 잘지키는 편인가요?
Do you tend to stick to your commitments?

가끔 기억을 못하거나 부득이한 사유로 인해서 약속을 못지키는 경우도 있어요. 그리고 저는 왠만하면 못지킬 약속은 잘 안하는 성격이예요.

9.6 약속을 잘지키는 편인가요?
Do you tend to stick to your commitments?

일에 있어서는 철저한 편입니다. 확실한 마감기간이 있다면 과정은 어찌되었든 마감은 지키는 것 같아요. 사람들과의 약속도 마찬가지입니다. 하지만 때로는 약속을 미루거나 취소하는 경우가 생기기도 합니다. 스스로 통제할 수 없는 상황이 생겼거나, 몸이 아플 경우에는 적어도 하루 전에는 상대방과 이야기하고 약속을 조율하는 것 같아요. 그리고 당일 약속시간은 특별한 일 없으면 조금 더 빨리 가거나 시간을 맞춥니다. 그래야 제 마음이 편안하고 안정적이기 때문입니다.

2B 능력

10.1 감정을 솔직하게 표현하는 편인가요?
Are you good at expressing how you feel?

감정 표현은 조금 서투른 편입니다. 저 스스로가 상대방의 입장을 먼저 생각하는 편입니다.

10.2 감정을 솔직하게 표현하는 편인가요?
Are you good at expressing how you feel?

네, 솔직하게 표현하는 편이지만, 가끔은 제 감정을 스스로 파악할 필요가 있어 감정표현에 시간이 좀 걸리는 편이에요. 특히 화가 나거나 섭섭한 마음이 들 때 말이에요.

10.3 감정을 솔직하게 표현하는 편인가요?
Are you good at expressing how you feel?

사람마다 다른 것 같아요. 감정을 솔직하게 표현해도 제 스스로가 안전하다고 느끼는 안전한 그룹이나 친구들에게는 이야기를 하는 편이지만, 직장동료들 또는 일로 만나는 사이나 가족이여도 부모님들께는 솔직한 감정을 표현하지 않는 편입니다. 예를 들면 부모님들께는 좋은 감정, 긍정적인 마음들은 나누지만 힘들고 어려운 부정적인 감정들은 나누지 않는 편입니다. 그 이유는 걱정하실 것 같아서 입니다. 그래서 늘 괜찮은 모습을 보이려고 하는 경향이 있습니다.

능력 2B

10.4 감정을 솔직하게 표현하는 편인가요?
Are you good at expressing how you feel?

어릴때는 제 감정을 솔직하게 표현했었어요. 하지만 나이가 들고 차츰 사회생활을 시작하면서 부터는 제 자신의 '감정'을 솔직하게 표현하는 것이 좋지 않다는 것을 경험했고, 가까운 지인들이나 가족들 외에의 타인에게는 감정 표현을 지양/자제 합니다.

10.5 감정을 솔직하게 표현하는 편인가요?
Are you good at expressing how you feel?

아니요. 어렸을때는 감정에 솔직 했더라면, 어느덧 30대 후반인 지금은 누구에게도 내 감정을 솔직히 표현하지 않는것 같아요. 아무래도 솔직히 표현함에 있어서 상처받고 신경쓸일이 많아지다보니 자연스럽게 그리 된 것 같습니다.

10.6 감정을 솔직하게 표현하는 편인가요?
Are you good at expressing how you feel?

아니요. 좀 더 어렸을 때는 그렇게 했던 것 같은데 나이를 먹으니 아무래도 솔직한 감정을 표현하는 것에 조심스럽게 되는 부분이 있어요. 또 가족에게는 긍정적이거나 부정적인 감정 모두 표현할 수 있지만, 가족 외의 사람에게 긍정적인 감정 외에 부정적인 감정을 표현하는 일이 많지는 않은 것도 같아요.

2B 능력

10.7 감정을 솔직하게 표현하는 편인가요?
Are you good at expressing how you feel?

아니요. 감정은 드러낼수록 약점이라고 생각하는 편이라 항상 감정 표현에 있어서는 다 드러내지 않는 편이에요.

10.8 감정을 솔직하게 표현하는 편인가요?
Are you good at expressing how you feel?

네. 전 정말 감정을 못 숨기는 편인 것 같아요. 그게 제 장점일 수도 있고 단점일 수도 있다고 생각해요. 그래도 다행인 점은 제가 일하는 분야는 자유로운 편이라 그런 것에 대한 스트레스가 일반 직장인 분들 보다는 덜하죠.

10.9 감정을 솔직하게 표현하는 편인가요?
Are you good at expressing how you feel?

상황에 따라 다른것 같아요. 주로 가족들이나 가까운 친구들에게는 감정을 솔직하게 표현하는 편이예요. 하지만 가까운 사람일수록 오히려 감정을 숨길때도 있어요. 왜냐하면 내 감정표현으로 상처를 받을까 걱정이 되기때문이예요. 그래서 저는 감정을 잘 통제하려 노력해요. 감정을 억제하려고 하기보다는 감정을 잘 표현하고 다스릴 수 있는 노력을 해요. 내 감정이 상황과 사람들을 불편하게 하지 않도록 노력하는 편이에요.

능력 2B

NOTES

2B 능력

NOTES

3A 습관에 대한 질문
QUESTIONS ABOUT HABITS

문법

~을/를 때

TO TALK ABOUT THINGS YOU DO WHEN DOING OTHER THINGS

WATCH A VIDEO LESSON!
Video: **Learn Korean | Korean Grammar 90: A/V-을 때/ㄹ 때**

Channel: 베이직 코리안 Basic Korean
TOPIK: 2급 (초급)

This grammar form can be attached to action verbs (동사) and descriptive verbs (형용사)
- Use ~을 때 when the verb (동사/형용사) ends in a final consonant (받침)
- Use ~를 때 when the verb (동사/형용사) does not end in a final consonant (받침)
- Use only 때 after a noun (명사)
- Use ~았/었을 때 to talk about things you did in the past

Used for talking about habits and things you do

한국에 갈 때 한국어로 말해요.	When I go to Korea I speak Korean.
머리가 아플 때 물을 마셔요.	When my head hurts I drink water.
저는 잘 때 꿈을 꾸지 않아요.	When I sleep I don't dream.
한국어를 말할 때 실수하는 것을 싫어해요.	When I speak Korean I hate making mistakes.
어렸을 때 차 멀미를 자주 했어요.	I often got carsick when I was a kid.

문법

~(으)ㄴ/는 편이다

TO TALK ABOUT HOW THINGS TEND TO BE (COMPARED TO OTHER THINGS)

WATCH A VIDEO LESSON!
Video: VS은/ㄴ/는 편이다 grammar / Intermediate Level / 한국어 연습해요 / 듣기 연습 /
Channel: 김선생님
TOPIK: 3급 (고급)

This grammar form can be attached to action verbs (동사) and descriptive verbs (형용사)
  Use ~는 편이다 when attaching to an action verb (동사)
  Use ~은 편이다 when attaching to a descriptive verb (형용사) with a final consonant
  Use ~ㄴ 편이다 when attaching to a 형용사 without a final consonant (받침)
  Use ~(으)ㄴ/는 편이 안이다 for things that tend not to be, or that you tend not to do.
  Use ~(으)ㄴ/는 편이었다 for things that tended to happen in the past
Used to talk about tendencies, and to make a sentence less direct

저는 공부를 잘 하는 편이에요.	I tend to study well.
이 영화가 지루한 편이에요.	This movie is on the boring side.
저는 게으른 편은 아니에요. 부지런한 편이죠.	I tend not to be lazy. I'm a pretty hard worker, you know.
어제 먹은 햄버거는 비싼 편이었어요.	The hamburger I ate yesterday was on the expensive side.

3A 습관

담배를 피나요? 담배를 피는 것에 대해 어떻게 생각하나요?
Do you smoke? How do you feel about smoking?

술을 마시나요? 음주 문화에 대해 어떻게 생각하나요?
Do you drink? How do you feel about drinking culture?

비흡연자 a nonsmoker | 흡연자 a smoker | 골초 a chain smoker | 담배를 끊다 to stop smoking | 술고래 a heavy drinker | 술자리 a drinking party | 취하다 to be drunk | 알딸딸하다 to be tipsy | 술 깨다 to sober up | 혼술하다 to drink alone | 숙취 a hangover

습관 3A

현재 복용중인 약이 있나요?
Do you take any medication?

혹시 블로그를 운영하고 있나요? 있다면 어떤 블로그 인가요?
Do you have a blog? If so, what is it about?

비타민제 vitamins | 보충하다 to supplement | 처방약 prescription drugs | 복용하다 to take a drug / a dose | 브이로그 a vlog | 일상 생활 daily life | 광고인 an advertiser | (온라인에) 올리다 to post (online) | 영양가 없는 포스트 a shitpost |

3A 습관

저녁 식탁에서 가장 흔한 대화 주제는 무엇이에요?
What is the most common conversation topic at your dinner table?

집에 있는 물건이 고장나면 보통 그것을 고치는 편이에요? 아니면 사는 편이에요?
When something in your home breaks, do you fix it or do you buy a new one?

봤던 드라마나 영화 등을 다시 보는 것을 좋아해요?
Do you like to rewatch TV shows, movies, etc?

일상적이다 to be routine/everyday | 평범하다 to be ordinary | 교체하다 to replace | 수다를 떨다 to gossip, to chat | 의논하다 to discuss | 위로가 되다 to be comforting | 배경으로 하다 to do sth in the background |

습관 3A

혹시 운동하나요? 주로 어떻게 운동해요?
Do you exercise? If so, how?

LISTEN TO NATIVE SPEAKERS!

Video: **연애보다 헬스?! 남녀가 운동에 미친 이유**
Working out over dating?! Reasons why men and women are crazy about exercize

Channel: 이십세들 (Twenty Birds)

Level: 고급 (Advanced)

근육 muscle | 헬스 / 헬스장 fitness center | 헬스하다 to go to the gym | 트레이너 a trainer | 무게 weight | 스트레스 해소 stress relief | 자존감 self-esteem |

3A 습관

길거리에 보이는 노숙자들에게 돈을 주나요?
Do you give money to homeless people you see on the street?

잠 들면서 어떤 생각을 하나요?
What do you think about when you're falling asleep?

잠꼬대를 하나요? 잠꼬대하면서 부끄러운 말을 해 본 적이 있나요?
Do you talk in your sleep? Have you ever said anything embarrassing?

기부하다 to donate | 무시하다 to ignore | 연민을 느끼다 to feel pity | 고민하다 to fret over | 생각이 떠오르다 to have thoughts come to your mind | 섬뜩하다 to be creepy | 웃기다 to be funny | 중얼거리다 to mumble | 횡설수설하다 to speak gibberish |

습관 3A

얼마나 많은 모자를 가지고 있어요?
How many hats do you own?

얼마나 많은 신발을 가지고 있어요?
How many shoes do you own?

신발을 신는 것과 맨발로 걷는 것 중 어떤 것을 더 좋아해요? Do you prefer to wear shoes or go barefoot?

항상 어울리는 양말을 신어요?
Do you always wear matching socks?

밟다 to step on sth | 꼼꼼하다 to be meticulous | 상관없다 to not matter |

3A 습관

코피를 어떻게 멈추나요?
How do you stop a bloody nose?

딸꾹질을 어떻게 멈추나요?
How do you stop hiccups?

식물을 어떻게 키우나요?
How do you care for a plant?

고개를 뒤로 젖히다 tilt one's head back | 막다 to plug up | 꼬집다 to pinch | 딸꾹질을 하다 to get hiccups | 숨을 멈추다 / 참다 to hold one's breath | 설탕 한 숟가락 a spoonful of sugar | 꾸준히 regularly | 화분 a flower pot | 다듬다 to prune | 확인하다 to check |

습관 — 3A

코를 골아요? 코고는 사람을 아세요?

Do you snore? Do you know somebody that does?

샤워하면서 노래해요? 샤워하면서 노래하는 사람을 아세요?

Do you sing in the shower? Do you know somebody that does?

드르렁거리다 to snore (lit. the sound of snoring) | 돼지처럼 코를 골다 to snore like a pig | 돌아눕다 to turn over | 팔꿈치로 치다 / 찌르다 to elbow | 음질 sound quality | 음향 acoustics | 개인적이다 personal/private |

3A 습관

배 멀미를 하나요? 배 멀미 했던 경험을 이야기 해보세요.
Do you get seasick? Talk about a time when you got seasick.

차 멀미를 하나요? 차 멀미 했던 경험을 이야기 해보세요.
Do you get carsick? Talk about a time when you got carsick.

배를 타다 to ride a boat | 흔들리다 to rock/to sway | 멀미약 pills for motion sickness | 속이 울렁거리다 to feel nauseous/queasy | 토하다 to throw up | 구불구불한 길 a winding road | 창밖을 보다 to look out the window |

습관 3A

구름에서 모양을 찾는 것을 좋아하나요?
Do you like to look for shapes in clouds?

별 보는 것을 좋아하세요?
Do you like stargazing?

중요한 프로젝트를 할 때 어떤 것에서 아이디어를 얻나요?
How do you find ideas when working on an important project?

상상하다 to imagine | 들어눕다 to lie down | 생생한 상상 a vivid imagination | 별자리 a constellation | 마음속에 그려 보다 to visualize | 영감을 받다 to get inspiration | 멍때리다 to space out | 토론하다 to discuss | 브레인스토밍을 하다 to brainstorm |

3A 습관

총을 갖고 있어요? 그렇지 않다면 언젠가 총을 구입하고 싶나요?
Do you own a gun? If not, do you want to buy one someday?

정리정돈을 잘 하는 편인가요? 아니면 지저분한 편인가요?
Do you tend to be tidy? If not, do you tend to be messy?

친구랑 만나면 보통 무엇을 하나요?
What do you and your friends usually do when you hang out?

사냥총 a hunting gun | 총기 소지증 a gun license | 즐기다 to enjoy | 신나다 to be exciting |
꿀잼 to be lots of fun (slang) |

습관 — 3A

나쁜 습관이 있나요?
Do you have any bad habits?

어렸을 때 어떤 버릇을 가지고 있었나요?
What habits did you have as a child that you have grown out of?

그만두다 to quit | 버릇을 고치다 to mend one's ways | 없어지다 to go away/to disappear | 의지력 willpower | 긴장성 행동 a nervous habit |

3A 습관

파란색 펜과 검정색 펜중 어떤 것이 더 좋으세요?
Do you prefer blue or black pens?

꼭 해야 하는 일을 메모하거나 리스트를 만드는 편인가요?
Do you make to-do lists?

가장 많이 사용하는 휴대폰 어플은 무엇인가요?
What's your most used phone app?

우선순위를 매기다 to prioritize | 체크하다 to check off | 부지런하다 to be diligent |
잊어버리다 to forget | 쓸모있다 to be useful | 시간을 보내다 to spend time |

습관 3A

행운의 부적이 있나요?
Do you have any "lucky" items?

무엇을 수집하나요?
Do you collect anything?

중고로 사고 싶은 것이 있나요?
Is there anything you prefer to buy second-hand?

집을 나설 때 호신용품을 챙기나요?
Do you carry anything with you for self-defence when you leave your house?

지니고 다니다 to carry around | 보호하다 to protect | 수집품 a collection | 품질 quality | 특별하다 to be special | 절약하다 to save money | 페퍼 스프레이 pepper spray |

3A 습관

당신은 안경을 써야 하나요? 안경을 쓰고 싶나요?
Do you need glasses? Do you want to wear glasses?

Video: LISTEN TO NATIVE SPEAKERS!
남녀가 안경을 벗으면 달라지는 이유
Why men and women change when they take off their glasses

Channel: 이십세들 (Twenty Birds)
Level: 고급 (Advanced)

잘생기다 to be handsome | 멋있다 to be cool | 유행 a fashion trend | 시력검사 an eye test | 시력검사판 an eye test chart | 가자미눈하다 to squint when you can't see sth clearly | 가짜안경 fake glasses |

습관 — 3A

잠을 잘 때 어떤 자세로 자나요? 옆을 보거나 똑바로 누워 자나요? 아니면 엎드려서 자나요?
When you sleep, do you usually sleep on your back, front, or side?

무엇으로 하루를 시작해요?
What do you do to start your day?

아침에 샤워하는 것과 저녁에 샤워하는 것 중에 어떤 것을 선호해요?
Do you prefer to shower in the mornings or evenings?

목 근육에 쥐가 나다 to have a crick in one's neck | 편안하다 to be comfortable | 베개 a pillow | 제일 먼저 first of all | 침대 정리하다 to make the bed | 땀이 나다 to sweat | 상황에 따라 다르다 to depend on the situation |

3A 습관

가장 싫어하는 집안일은 무엇인가요?
What chore do you most hate doing?

집에 오면 제일 먼저 하는 일이 뭐예요?
What's the first thing you do when you get home?

자기 전에 하는 루틴이 있나요?
Do you have a bedtime routine?

미루게되다 to put off doing | 귀찮다 to be a pain/to be a drag | 빨래를 개다 to fold laundry |
피하다 to avoid | 푹 쉬다 to get a good rest | 바로 right away |

습관 3A

건강한 생활을 위해서 어떤 생활방식을 바꿔 보았나요?
What healthy lifestyle change(s) have you made?

....

....

....

....

....

....

더 건강해지기 위해 할 수 있는 일은 무엇인가요?
What are some things you could do to be healthier?

....

....

....

....

....

....

증가하다 to increase | 감소하다 to decrease | 조절하다 to control/regulate | 노력하다 to make an effort | 습관을 기르다 to develop a habit | 연구하다 to research |

3A 습관

꿈해몽을 하나요?
Do you look for meaning in your dreams?

운전 중에 차가 막힐 때 보통 차안에서 무엇을 하나요?
What do you do when you're stuck in traffic?

다른 사람들과 나누고 싶은 것들이 있나요?
What are some things that you like to share with other people?

꿈해몽/꿈풀이 a dream interpretation | 상징 symbolism | 주제 theme | 미래를 예언하다 to fortell the future | 짜증이 나다 to be annoyed | 지루하다 to be bored | 노잼 to be no fun (slang) | 손이 크다 to be a big spender | 마음이 넓다 to be generous | 구두쇠 a cheapskate |

습관 3A

파티를 여는 것을 좋아하세요?
Do you like to throw parties?

요즘 뭔가 마음에 걸리는 일이 있나요?
What's on your mind these days?

미신을 믿나요? 중요한 날에 피하는 징크스가 있나요? Are you superstitious? Is there anything you do to avoid getting 'jinxes' on important days?

축하하다 to celebrate | 초대하다 to invite | 준비하다 to prepare | 일부러 on purpose | 우연히 by accident | 미신에 따르다 according to superstition |

3A 습관

예산을 관리하시나요?
Do you keep a budget?

돈을 절약해야 할 때 어디부터 비용을 줄여요?
Where do you cut costs when you need to save money?

계산하다 to calculate | 낭비 a waste | 예산을 짜다 to make a budget | 생활비 cost of living |

습관 3A

돈이 없음에도 불구하고 분수에 맞지 않은 삶을 살고 있나요?
Do you spend money you don't have, or live beyond your means?

은퇴 후를 위해 돈을 모으고 있나요? 모으지 않는다면 아직 돈을 벌 수 있는 시간이 있다고 생각하시나요?
Are you saving for retirement? If not, do you think you still have time?

과소비 overspending | 빚을 지다 to fall into debt | 카드빚 credit card debt | 무모하다 to be reckless | 어쩔수 없다 it can't be helped | 연금 a pension | 퇴직금 severance pay | 은퇴 계획 a retirement plan |

3A 습관

한국어를 어떻게 공부하나요?
How do you study Korean?

주로 mostly, mainly, primarily | 열심히 diligently | 틈만 나면 하다 to do when you have a chance | 마음대로 as one likes |

3B 습관에 대한 원어민 답변예시

NATIVE KOREAN WRITING SAMPLES

3B 습관

11.01 가장 싫어하는 집안일이 무엇인가요?
What chore do you most hate doing?

저는 설거지 하는 것을 가장 싫어합니다. 맛있는 음식을 요리하고 먹는 것은 좋은데 싱크대가 너무 낮아 허리가 아파요. 또 싱크대가 낮아 물이 옷에 튀어 설거지를 하고 나면 옷을 갈아입어야합니다.

11.02 가장 싫어하는 집안일이 무엇인가요?
What chore do you most hate doing?

딱히 싫어하는 집안일은 없지만, 대청소는 귀찮을 때가 있어요. 대청소 때 창문 유리, 매트나 카펫 청소, 가구 밑 먼지 쓸기 등등은 시간이 오래 걸리니까 좀 하기 싫어서 미루게 돼요.

11.03 가장 싫어하는 집안일이 무엇인가요?
What chore do you most hate doing?

물건을 이것저것 많이 사는편이라 정리하는게 제일 싫어요! 일주일에 한번씩 하곤하는데 할 때마다 힘들어요.

11.04 가장 싫어하는 집안일이 무엇인가요?
What chore do you most hate doing?

설거지입니다. 한 자리에 계속 서있어야 하고 그릇이 깨질까봐 조심스러워지는 것이 스트레스를 주기 때문입니다.

습관 3A

11.05 가장 싫어하는 집안일이 무엇인가요?
What chore do you most hate doing?

전 설거지가 그렇게 귀찮더라고요... 저는 만사가 귀찮아서 평소에 설거지 할 때 앞치마도 안하고 하는데요, 온몸에 물이 튀어 옷이 다 젖어서 짜증이 날 때가 많아요. 하지만 어쩌겠어요... 설거지를 안해놓으면 나중에 접시가 필요할 때 곤란해 지거든요.

11.06 가장 싫어하는 집안일이 무엇인가요?
What chore do you most hate doing?

집안일 자체가 그냥 싫은데ㅋㅋ 큐ㅠ 청소기 돌리는 걸 유독 싫어합니다. 왜냐하면 어렸을 때부터 청소기 돌리다가 그 청소기 줄이랑 청소기에 발을 부딪히는 일이 많아서....크게 다치진 않았지만 그 왠지 모를 아픔 아시죠??ㅋㅋㅋ

11.07 가장 싫어하는 집안일이 무엇인가요?
What chore do you most hate doing?

저는 사실 집안일은 다 싫어하는데, 빨래 개는 게 제일 싫어요. 앉아서 개든 서서 개든 심지어 누워서 개든 허리가 너무 아프고 내가 뭘 하는 건지도 모르겠고 갠 빨래를 옷장에 넣는 것도 귀찮아요. 차라리 빨래를 하는 것 자체는 나은데 하고 나서 개는 게 너무 싫네요.

3B 습관

11.08 가장 싫어하는 집안일이 무엇인가요?
What chore do you most hate doing?

저도 설거지를 싫어해요. 미뤄두면 나중에 더 하기 싫어져서 요리중 사용한 그릇은 바로바로 씻는 편입니다.

11.09 가장 싫어하는 집안일이 무엇인가요?
What chore do you most hate doing?

빨래널기다. 엄마한테서 꾸준히 들어온 잔소리가 '빨래 널어라'였다. 그 때문에 빨래 너는 것은 웬만하면 피하려고 한다. 크게 힘들지 않고 금방 끝나는 일인데도 말이다.

11.10 가장 싫어하는 집안일이 무엇인가요?
What chore do you most hate doing?

방청소가 제일 자신 없습니다. 싫어하지는 않지만 방 청소는 하기전과 하고나서의 차이를 알아보기 힘들고, 내 기준에는 깨끗하게 된것 같은데 남이볼 땐 아직 청소가 덜 된거같은 그런 결과가 자주 나와서 좋아하지 않습니다. 그에 비해 결과가 눈에 바로 보이는 빨래, 욕실청소, 설거지는 좋아합니다

습관 3A

12.01 무엇으로 하루를 시작해요?
What do you do to start your day?

아침에 그냥 일어나기 싫다 하면서 일어나는데...

12.02 무엇으로 하루를 시작해요?
What do you do to start your day?

머리감기!! 잠도 깰겸 하루를 시작한다는 기분을 주기 때문이죠.

12.03 무엇으로 하루를 시작해요?
What do you do to start your day?

아침에 일어나자마자 항상 침대 정리를 바로 해요. 이불과 베개를 깔끔하게 정리해요.

12.04 무엇으로 하루를 시작해요?
What do you do to start your day?

침대에서 일어나기 전, 남자친구한테 아침 인사 문자를 보내는 것으로 시작합니다

3B 습관

12.05 무엇으로 하루를 시작해요?
What do you do to start your day?

누워서 핸드폰을 한 시간 정도 하네요.... 고쳐야 하는데.

12.06 무엇으로 하루를 시작해요?
What do you do to start your day?

한 컵의 물입니다. 건강에 좋다는 이야기를 들은 탓도 있고, 실제로도 잠이 좀 깨거든요.

12.07 무엇으로 하루를 시작해요?
What do you do to start your day?

눈 뜨면 먼저 양치를 하고 세수를 한뒤 물을 마십니다. 아침은 거의 먹지 않고 가끔 시리얼이나 빵으로 대신합니다. 그리고는 옷을 입고 바로 출근합니다

12.08 무엇으로 하루를 시작해요?
What do you do to start your day?

아침을 먹습니다. 헬스를 하는 날에는 단백질 위주의 식사를 합니다. 아닌 경우 저칼로리 음식을 먹습니다.

습관 3A

12.09 무엇으로 하루를 시작해요?
What do you do to start your day?

저는 아침에 집주변 강가를 산책하면서 하루를 시작해요. 아침공기를 마시면 상쾌하고 피로가 풀리는 느낌이 들거든요.

12.10 무엇으로 하루를 시작해요?
What do you do to start your day?

스마트폰 보기!!! 스마트폰으로 카카오톡이나 웹툰이나 커뮤니티 글, 교수님의 알림 등을 먼저 확인합니다.

12.11 무엇으로 하루를 시작해요?
What do you do to start your day?

저는 항상 샤워를 하며 하루를 시작합니다. 학교 수업을 가야하는데 바로 샤워를 하지 않으면 다시 잠이 들어 수업에 가지 못한 적이 있기 때문입니다.

12.12 무엇으로 하루를 시작해요?
What do you do to start your day?

평소엔 아침식사로 하루를 시작해요. 빵을 토스트기에 구워서 제가 직접 만든 오렌지잼을 발라먹고요, 그 다음엔 물을 뎁혀[1] 녹차를 우려 마셔요.

[1] 뎁히다 is Busan dialect for the standard word 데우다 meaning "to make something warm"

3B 습관

13.01 중요한 프로젝트를 할 때 어떤 것에서 아이디어를 얻나요? How do you find ideas when working on an important project?

그냥 멍때리다가 갑자기 떠오르는 아이디어를 적어두고 거기서 추려요.

13.02 중요한 프로젝트를 할 때 어떤 것에서 아이디어를 얻나요? How do you find ideas when working on an important project?

그림을 그릴 때는 주로 예전 여행 사진, 내가 좋아하는 컬러 조합 등, 지나간 자료들을 자주 훑어 본답니다.

13.03 중요한 프로젝트를 할 때 어떤 것에서 아이디어를 얻나요? How do you find ideas when working on an important project?

같이 프로젝트를 하는 사람들과 토론을 하면서 아이디어를 얻거나 기존에 비슷한 주제로 진행된 논문이 있는지 찾아봅니다.

13.04 중요한 프로젝트를 할 때 어떤 것에서 아이디어를 얻나요? How do you find ideas when working on an important project?

보통은 브레인스토밍을 많이 하는 것 같아요. 거기서 아이디어를 많이 만든 다음에 그 아이디어들을 정리하죠.

습관 3A

13.05 중요한 프로젝트를 할 때 어떤 것에서 아이디어를 얻나요?
How do you find ideas when working on an important project?

관련된 주제로 아무 얘기나 계속 하다가 괜찮아 보이는 거 있으면 적어둡니다. 하지만 대부분의 아이디어는 자신이 아는 범위 내에서 나오더라고요. 평소에 책도 많이 보고, 다른 분야의 지식도 계속 습득하는 습관을 들여야 합니다.

13.06 중요한 프로젝트를 할 때 어떤 것에서 아이디어를 얻나요?
How do you find ideas when working on an important project?

인터넷으로 알아본다. 특히 네이버 검색창으로. 인터넷은 온세상의 좋은 정보, 나쁜 정보가 다 담겨 있는 곳이라 모르는 부분이 있으면 무의식적으로 스마트폰 버튼을 누르게된다.

13.07 중요한 프로젝트를 할 때 어떤 것에서 아이디어를 얻나요?
How do you find ideas when working on an important project?

주로 상상속에서 아이디어를 얻어요. 업무에 대해 아무 생각 없을 때 제일 좋은 아이디어가 떠오를 때가 많기 때문에 창밖을 바라본다던지 샤워를 할 때 아이디어가 떠올라요.

3B 습관

13.08 중요한 프로젝트를 할 때 어떤 것에서 아이디어를 얻나요?
How do you find ideas when working on an important project?

저는 평소 생활에서 아이디어를 캐내는 편이에요. 제가 하는 일이 사람들의 공감을 얻어내는건데요, 많은 사람들의 공감을 이끌어내려면 모든 사람들이 겪을 법한 소소한 사건이나 이야기에서 아이디어를 얻어와 프로젝트에 적용시켜야해요.

13.09 중요한 프로젝트를 할 때 어떤 것에서 아이디어를 얻나요?
How do you find ideas when working on an important project?

우선은 나의 경험 속에서 찾습니다. 기억에 없거나 기억이 희미해진 것들은 예전 자료를 찾아봅니다. 여전히 답을 찾을 수 없다면 선배들이나 해결책을 알 것 같은 사람에게 자문을 구합니다. 세상에 온전히 새로운 것은 그다지 많지 않기 때문이죠.

13.10 중요한 프로젝트를 할 때 어떤 것에서 아이디어를 얻나요?
How do you find ideas when working on an important project?

아이디어를 짜내려고 머리를 계속 써서 여러개를 떠올리는 것 보다는 처음에 떠오른 몇 개를 가지고 시간을 두고 깊게 생각합니다. 잠깐 휴식을 하거나 일부러 다른일을 하면서 생각이 한 쪽으로 매몰되지 않게끔 노력도 하구요.

습관 3A

14.01 미신을 믿나요? 중요한 날에 하는 어떤 징크스가 있나요? Are you superstitious? Is there anything you [...]

미신을 믿지 않습니다. 따라서 징크스도 없습니다. 중요한 날에는 마음을 다잡아서 하루를 잘 보내려고 노력합니다.

14.02 미신을 믿나요? 중요한 날에 하는 어떤 징크스가 있나요? Are you superstitious? Is there anything you [...]

미신은 아니지만 중요한 일이 있으면 그 전날 깨끗하게 몸을 씻는 편이예요. 목욕을 할수 있으면 목욕도 하고요.

14.03 미신을 믿나요? 중요한 날에 하는 어떤 징크스가 있나요? Are you superstitious? Is there anything you [...]

미신을 믿지 않고 징크스도 딱히 없긴 한데, 중요한 시험 앞두고 미역국을 먹지 말라는 말이 있어서 굳이 먹지는 않습니다.

14.04 미신을 믿나요? 중요한 날에 하는 어떤 징크스가 있나요? Are you superstitious? Is there anything you [...]

미신을 믿는 편은 아니고, 중요한 날 어떤 징크스도 없지만 가끔 아침 일찍 유리, 거울, 도자기 컵 등이 깨지면 기분이 좀 안좋고, 오늘 하루 좀 조심해야겠다 라는 생각이 들어요.

3B 습관

14.05 미신을 믿나요? 중요한 날에 하는 어떤 징크스가 있나요? Are you superstitious? Is there anything you [...]

시험 보기 전에 초콜릿을 먹는다던지 나쁜 꿈을 꾸면 하루는 조심한다던지 중요한 일 전에 미역국은 먹으면 안된다 던지 그런 거는 딱히 믿지는 않아도 따르게 되는 거 같아요!

14.06 미신을 믿나요? 중요한 날에 하는 어떤 징크스가 있나요? Are you superstitious? Is there anything you [...]

미신을 딱히 믿지는 않아요. 하지만 유명한 징크스에 해당하는 일이 있다면 무슨 일이 생기려나? 하고 걱정을 하고는 해요.

14.07 미신을 믿나요? 중요한 날에 하는 어떤 징크스가 있나요? Are you superstitious? Is there anything you [...]

믿지 않습니다. 시험날에 미역국 먹으면 떨어진다는 미신이 있지만 마침 생일이라 아침에 미역국 먹고 시험쳐서 딴 자격증도 있습니다.

14.08 미신을 믿나요? 중요한 날에 하는 어떤 징크스가 있나요? Are you superstitious? Is there anything you [...]

그렇기도 하고 그렇지 않기도 합니다. 정말 간절할 정도로 중요한 일을 앞두게 되면 기도를 하는 경우가 있습니다. 심리적으로 기댈 곳을 찾게 되는게 원인인 것 같습니다. 종교처럼요.

습관 3A

14.09 미신을 믿나요? 중요한 날에 하는 어떤 징크스가 있나요? Are you superstitious? Is there anything you do to avoid 'jinxes' on important days?

아뇨 저는 잘은 믿지 않는 편이에요. 딱 하나 있는 것 같은데요, 날씨와 시험 사이의 상관성이네요. 전에 봤던 시험날에 비가왔었는데 그 시험 성적이 좋았다면, 이번 시험때에도 비가 온다면 운이 좋겠거니 믿는편이에요. 얼추 들어맞는 것같더라구요!

14.10 미신을 믿나요? 중요한 날에 하는 어떤 징크스가 있나요? Are you superstitious? Is there anything you do to avoid 'jinxes' on important days?

평생 미신을 안 믿는다고 생각했는데 점점 믿게 되네요. 시험날에 미역국을 안 먹는 건 물론이고 의자를 빼고 자거나 하지도 않아요.① 집 인테리어를 할 때도 거울은 현관을② 마주보는 곳에 있지 않아야 한다거나, 돈과 칼은 숨겨두고, 이사는 손 없는 날에 하고③ 그러네요.

14.11 미신을 믿나요? 중요한 날에 하는 어떤 징크스가 있나요? Are you superstitious? Is there anything you do to avoid 'jinxes' on important days?

완전히 믿는것은 아니지만, 그래도 지켜서 나쁠건 없다는 생각으로 일부러 빨간색으로④ 이름을 적는다던지 문지방에 올라선다든지 해서 어기지는 않습니다.⑤ 널리 알려진 미신은 아니지만, 중요한날에는 균형을 맞추려고 합니다, 뭐 시험치는 날에 난간을 왼손으로 잡았다면, 일부러 오른손으로 한번 잡아주는 방식으로요.

[1] 의자를 빼고 자다 - sleeping with a chair pulled away from the desk will invited ghosts to sit.
[2] 거울은 현관을 마주보다 - having a mirror face the entryway creates bad energy [feng shui]
[3] 손 없는 날 - days without "손" (evil spirits); days ending in a 0 or 9 on the lunar calendar

3B 습관

15.01 더 건강해지기 위해 할 수 있는 일은 무엇인가요? What are some things you could do to be healthier?

아침에 일어나자마자 8분짜리 체조 영상을 따라한다. 그 다음에 씻고, 아침 식사로 사과 한 알을 먹는다.

15.02 더 건강해지기 위해 할 수 있는 일은 무엇인가요? What are some things you could do to be healthier?

식습관 개선입니다. 저는 고기 위주의 식사를 하는데, 채소를 좀 더 먹을 필요가 있습니다

15.03 더 건강해지기 위해 할 수 있는 일은 무엇인가요? What are some things you could do to be healthier?

규칙적인 수면을 하고, 운동을 꾸준히 하며, 스트레스를 덜 받도록 노력해야합니다.

15.04 더 건강해지기 위해 할 수 있는 일은 무엇인가요? What are some things you could do to be healthier?

달리기가 가장 좋은 것 같습니다. 개인적인 경험 때문인데, 달리기로 체중을 꽤 많이 줄여봤기 때문입니다. 비만은 세계 어디서나 건강의 적이거든요.

---

4 빨간색으로 이름을 적다 - red is associated with death, so writing a name in red is very unlucky
5 문지방에 올라선다 - stepping on the threshold of a doorway in a house is unlucky

습관 3A

15.05 더 건강해지기 위해 할 수 있는 일은 무엇인가요?
What are some things you could do to be healthier?

현재 한국에 입국해서 자가격리 중인데 자가격리가 끝나면 운동을 지속적으로 하려구요. 살이 많이 찌기도 했고 미국에서 한국으로 오기 전에 약 한달 반 정도를 운동했더니 정말 아침에 일어나는게 매우 수월했어요.

15.06 더 건강해지기 위해 할 수 있는 일은 무엇인가요?
What are some things you could do to be healthier?

핸드폰 덜 만지기가 일단 제일 중요할 것 같고 거기다 매일매일 운동하기 정도가 좋겠네요. 코로나 터지기 전에는 매일 운동을 갔는데 터진 후로는 정말 한 번도 운동을 안 했어요. 근육량이 줄어든 게 체감이 돼서 슬퍼요.

15.07 더 건강해지기 위해 할 수 있는 일은 무엇인가요?
What are some things you could do to be healthier?

적절한 운동과 적당한 휴. 그리고 맛있는 거 많이 먹기…..나만의 취미 만들기… 스트레스 받으면 그 스트레스를 없애려고 본인만의 해결방법이 있어야한다고 생각합니다. 저는 먹는 걸로 주로 푸는 사람이고, 요새는 SF나 추리소설을 읽으면서 풀고 있어요①

[1] SF is short for "science fiction (novel)"

3B 습관

15.08 더 건강해지기 위해 할 수 있는 일은 무엇인가요? What are some things you could do to be healthier?

매일 저녁 스트레칭을 해서 긴장되고 피곤한 몸과 근육을 풀어주려고 노력하고 있지만 잊어버리고 안할 때가 더 많아요.

15.09 더 건강해지기 위해 할 수 있는 일은 무엇인가요? What are some things you could do to be healthier?

집에 가만히 누워서 유튜브 보지말고 걷거나 자전거를 타야하는데, 마음만 먹고 실천을 안하고 있어서 죄책감이 느껴집니다.

15.10 더 건강해지기 위해 할 수 있는 일은 무엇인가요? What are some things you could do to be healthier?

예전에는 조깅을 꾸준히 했습니다, 조깅을 할 수없는 날에는 뒷산에 가거나 집에서 실내운동을 조금씩 했습니다. 스스로가 게으르다고 생각하기 때문에 운동에서 저의 제 1원칙은 무리하지 않는것 입니다. 선수가 아니기 때문에 기록에 목 맬 필요도 없으니 조금만 힘들것 같으면 그만두고, 다음에 다시 하는 방식으로 너무 힘들지 않게 매일매일 하는 방식을 선호하는데 그에 맞는 운동이 조깅이나 등산을 선호하고 종종 합니다

습관 3A

NOTES

3B 습관

NOTES

4A 여행에 대한 질문
QUESTIONS ABOUT TRAVEL

WATCH A VIDEO!

Video: 당신이 서울에서 꼭 가봐야 할 장소 10
10 places in Seoul you have to go to

Channel: Seoul Trip Walk

문법

~고 싶다

TO TALK ABOUT THINGS YOU WANT TO DO

WATCH A VIDEO LESSON!
Video: **Let's learn about 'V-고 싶다' in korean grammar. [ENG sub]**
Channel: 꼬미스쿨 GGOMI SCHOOL
TOPIK: 1급 (초급)

This grammar form can be attached to action verbs (동사).
    Use ~고 싶었다 to talk about things you wanted to do in the past
    Use ~고 싶어 하다 to talk about things somebody else wants to do
    Use with 안 or ~지 않다 to talk about things you don't want to do
When used with descriptive verbs (형용사) add the form -아/어/여지고 싶다.

내년에 한국에 가고 싶어요.	I want to go to Korea next year.
작년에 독일에서 여행하고 싶었어요.	I wanted to vacation in Germany last year.
제 언니가 일본에 가고 싶어 해요.	My older sister wants to go to Japan.
너무 추워서 안타르티카에 가고 싶지 않아요.	I don't want to go to Antarctica because it's too cold.
올 여름에는 비키니를 입기 위해 날씬해지고 싶어요.	I want to be skinny so I can wear my bikini this summer.

문법

~(으)려고 하다

TO TALK ABOUT THINGS YOU INTEND ON DOING

WATCH A VIDEO LESSON!

Video: 【한국어 초급 문법】-(으)려고 하다 Korean basic grammar 저는 주말에 친구를 만나려고 해요.
Channel: 한국어 한 조각 A Piece Of Korean
TOPIK: 1급 (초급)

This grammar form can be attached to action verbs (동사).
    Use ~으려고 하다 if the action verb (동사) ends in a final consonant (받침).
    Use ~려고 하다 if the action verb (동사) does not end in a final consonant (받침), or if the final consonant (받침) is ㄹ.
    Use ~(으)려고 했다 to talk about things you intended to do in the past.

이번 주말에 뉴욕에 가려고 해요.	I intend to go to New York this weekend.
한국에 가면 많이 먹으려고 해요.	I intend to eat a lot when I go to Korea.
호주에 혼자 살아 보려고 해요.	I intend to live alone in Australia.
비행기를 타려고 했어요.	I intended to take the plane.
이번 여름에는 여행하려고 했는데 코로나 때문에 갈 수 없었어요.	I intended to go on vacation this summer but because of COVID I couldn't go.
휴가 때는 회사에서 오는 연락은 받지 않으려고 해요.	I don't intend to accept any work messages during my vacation.

4A 여행

축제나 카니발에 갔었던 경험을 이야기 해 주세요.
Talk about a time you've gone to a festival or a carnival.

LISTEN TO NATIVE SPEAKERS!

Video: [국내여행] 열려라 바닷길!!! 두 발로 직접 바다를 건너다~! 진도 신비의 바닷길 축제

[Local Travel] Open up, sea road!!! Crossing the ocean on our own two feet~! The Jindo Miracle Sea Road Festival

Channel: 잼쏭부부 jemissong

Level: 중급 (Intermediate)

축제 현장 a festival venue/site | 유명하다 to be famous | 장화 rainboots | 딱딱하다 to be firm | 해가 뜨다 the sun rises | 보람이 있다 to be worth doing | 조개 a clam | 믿거나 말거나 believe it or not | 미역 seaweed | 다시마 kelp | 심봤다! jackpot! | 낭만적이다 to be romantic |

여행 4A

국적을 두개 가질 수 있다면, 어떤 나라의 국적을 취득하고 싶나요?
If you could have dual citizenship, what would the other country be?

일등석이나 비지니스석을 타 본 적이 있나요?
Have you ever traveled in first class or business class?

얼마나 많은 나라를 방문해 보았나요?
How many countries have you visited?

기회 an opportunity | 여권 a passport | 자유롭게 freely | 막힘 없이 without any obstacles | 출장 a business trip | 가난하다 to be poor | 좌석을 예약하다 to reserve a seat | 널찍하다 to be roomy/spacious | 원하다 to want/wish for | 자랑하다 to show off/to brag |

4A 여행

휴가 때 주로 하는 것은 무엇인가요?
What do you mostly do when you're on vacation?

마지막으로 여행했던 장소는 어디인가요?
Where was the last place you traveled to?

관광을 하다 to go sightseeing | 유적지 historical sights | 명소 a sight/attraction |
돌아다니다 to wander around | 답사하다 / 탐험하다 to explore | 방문하다 to visit |
묵다 to stay | 숙박 an accommodation |

여행 4A

여긴 정말 꼭 가 봐야 한다는 장소가 있나요?
Where is a place you think everyone should visit?

여자친구나 남자친구랑 같이 여행을 해 본 적이 있나요? 그 여행은 어땠어요?
Have you ever traveled with a boyfriend or girlfriend? How did it go?

딱히 없다 nothing in particular | 추천하다 to recommend | 기억에 남다 to be memorable | 특히 especially | 대판 싸우다 to have a big fight | 친하다 to be close (emotionally) | 잘 어울리다 to be matched well | 서로 eachother |

4A 여행

해외 여행을 해 본 적이 있나요?
Have you traveled abroad?

해외 여행을 하면서 본 것 중에 가장 이상했던 것은 무엇이었나요?
What was the strangest thing you saw on your trip?

추수감사절에는 주로 무엇을 해요?
What do you usually do for Thanksgiving?

국내 domestic | 국제 international | 멀다 to be far | 여러나라 various countries | 칠면조 a turkey | 퍼레이드를 보다 to watch a parade | 미식축구 american football | 크렌베리 cranberry | 감사해야 할 일 sth to be thankful for |

여행 4A

기회가 생긴다면 우주로 여행을 갈 것 같아요?
Would you travel to space if you had the chance?

화성에서 살 수 있을 것 같아요?
Do you think you could live on Mars?

특이한 여행 습관을 가지고 있나요?
Do you have any unusual travel habits?

무중력 zero gravity | 지구 earth | 우주선 a space ship | 우주 비행사 an astronaut | 외롭다 to be lonely | 영원히 forever | 기온이 영하이다 to have freezing temperatures | 존재하다 to exist

4A 여행

장거리 여행 시 기차와 비행기 중에 어떤 교통수단을 선호하나요?
Would you rather take a long train ride or a long plane ride?

_____

_____

_____

_____

_____

_____

_____

차를 타고 가 본 것 중에 가장 긴 여행은 무엇이었어요? 어디에 다녀 왔나요?
What was the longest road trip you've ever taken in a car? Where did you go?

_____

_____

_____

_____

_____

_____

_____

답답하다 to be stuffy/stifling | 풍경 scenery (versatile) | 경치 scenery (landscape) |
불편하다 uncomfortable/inconvenient | 휴게소 a rest stop | 과자 a snack |
로드트립을 가다 to go on a road trip | 무사히 to be safe/without incident |

159

여행 4A

어떻게 명절 기분을 느끼나요?
How do you get into the holiday spirit?

방랑자처럼 정착하지 않고 여행하는 삶에 대해 어떻게 생각하세요?
What do you think about the vagabond lifestyle?

지금까지 타봤던 교통수단 중에 가장 이상하고 재미있었던 것은 뭐예요?
What is the strangest/most interesting transportation you've ever ridden on?

꾸미다 to decorate | 세우다 to set up | 명절 기분을 갖다 to have holiday cheer | 구상하다 to map/to plan out | 모험을 떠나다 to go on an adventure | 애매하다 to be vague/ambiguous/uncertain | 방랑자적이다 to be nomadic |

4A 여행

여행을 갈 때 기념품을 사는 편이에요?
Do you buy souvenirs when you go traveling?

여행을 가서 엽서를 보내는 편이예요?
Do you send post cards when you go traveling?

한국에 가 본 적이 있나요?
Have you ever been to Korea?

알뜰하다 to be frugal | 서울타워 Seoul Tower | 경복궁 the main royal palace in Seoul | 한옥마을 traditional Korean village | 한복 traditional korean clothes | 한식 korean food |

여행 4A

혼자서 여행을 해 본 적이 있나요? 그 여행은 어땠어요?
Have you ever traveled solo? How did it go?

여행을 할 때 새로운 사람을 만나는 것을 좋아하나요?
Do you like to meet new people when you go traveling?

독립적이다 to be independent | 안전하다 to be safe | 결정하다 to decide | 친하다 to be friendly

4A 여행

여행을 갈 때 현지 음식을 먹어 보는 편이에요?
Do you like to try the local food when you travel?

여행을 가서 먹어 봤던 가장 이상한 음식은 뭐예요?
What's the most unusual food you've tried while traveling?

식중독 food poisoning | 현지인 a local person | 특별식 a specialty food | 별미 a delicacy |
모험이 되다 to be adventurous | 뱉어 내다 to spit sth out | 포장마차 a food stall |

여행 4A

현지 언어를 할 줄 모르는 곳을 여행해 본 적이 있나요? 어땠나요?
Have you traveled somewhere where you didn't speak the language? How did it go?

여행을 할 때 관광객이 많은 곳은 피하시나요?
When you travel, do you avoid places with lots of tourists?

말이 통하다 to speak the same language | 불만이 있다 to have a complaint | 당황하다 to be embarrassing | 착각하다 to be mistaken / misunderstand | 관광객에게 인기 있다 to be popular with tourists | 붐비다 to be bustling | 성수기 peak season | 비수기 off season |

4A 여행

여름에 하는 가장 좋아하는 활동이 뭐예요?
What are your favorite summer activities?

겨울에 하는 가장 좋아하는 활동이 뭐예요?
What are your favorite winter activities?

가을에 하는 가장 좋아하는 활동이 뭐예요?
What are your favorite autumn activities?

봄에 하는 가장 좋아하는 활동이 뭐예요?
What are your favorite spring activities?

더위를 식히다 to cool off | 단풍이 들다 the leaves change color | 꽃이 피다 the flowers bloom | 눈에서 / 눈속에서 놀다 to play in the snow |

여행 4A

가장 기억에 남는 여름방학은 무엇인가요?
What is your most memorable summer vacation?

가장 기억에 남는 겨울방학은 무엇인가요?
What is your most memorable winter vacation?

잊을 수 없다 to be unforgettable | 처음으로 for the first time | 꿈만 같다 to be like a dream | 믿기지 않다 to be unbelievable | 숨이 멎는 줄 알았다 to be breathtaking | 실감이 안 나다 to not feel real / to not have sunk in |

4A 여행

여행할 때 하루에 얼마나 많은 돈을 쓰나요?
When you travel, how much do you usually spend per day?

전용기를 갖고 싶어요? 럭셔리 요트를 갖고 싶어요? Would you rather have a private jet or a luxury yacht?

여행할 때 여행 비용을 줄일 수 있는 꿀팁이 있나요?
Do you have any tricks to cut costs when you travel?

여행 비용 travel expenses | 포함하다 to include | 제외하다 to exclude | 할인 a discount | 패키지 여행 a package trip |

여행 　4A

공항에 가는 것을 좋아하나요?
Do you like going to airports?

가장 별로 였던 휴가는 언제인가요? 어떤 일이 있었나요?
What is your worst vacation memory? What happened?

복잡하다 to be crowded | 줄을 서서 기다리다 to wait in line | 서두르다 to hurry | 깔끔하다 to be neat / tidy | 지나가는 사람들 구경하기 people-watching | 바가지를 쓰다 to get/be ripped off | 아쉽다 to be a shame | 안타깝다 to be a pity | 끔찍하다 to be terrible |

4A 여행

당신의 고향에 놀러가는 관광객을 위해서 여정을 짜 보세요.
Plan a fun itinerary for a tourist visiting your hometown.

막상 actually / ultimately | 그나마 even so / nevertheless | 심지어 to even do sth |
아무래도 [아무리 생각해도] somehow / the way I see it... |

4B 여행에 대한 원어민 답변예시

NATIVE KOREAN WRITING SAMPLES

Note: these responses were collected in May 2021, during the Coronavirus pandemic.

4B 여행

16.1 휴가 때 주로 하는 것은 무엇인가요?
What do you mostly do when you're on vacation?

볼거리가 많은 곳이라면 성실히 돌아다니고, 편히 쉴 수 있는 휴양지라면 수영장에서 놀고 맛있는거 먹는건 둘다 빠지지 않죠

16.2 휴가 때 주로 하는 것은 무엇인가요?
What do you mostly do when you're on vacation?

해외여행 가는걸 좋아해요. 호텔보다는 저렴한 게스트하우스나 호스텔에서 묵고 아낀 돈으로 술 먹는데 씁니다

16.3 휴가 때 주로 하는 것은 무엇인가요?
What do you mostly do when you're on vacation?

평소에는 그저 집에서 뒹굴뒹굴하는걸 좋아합니다. 저는 아무 생각 안하고 가만히 있는게 제일 좋아요. 머리도 휴식할 시간을 줘야죠 ㅋㅋ

16.4 휴가 때 주로 하는 것은 무엇인가요?
What do you mostly do when you're on vacation?

'여기가 가고 싶다' 하는 곳이 없다면 집 안에만 있습니다. 그렇게 휴가를 보내고 돌아다니지 않은 걸 후회하죠 ㅠㅠ

여행 4B

16.5 휴가 때 주로 하는 것은 무엇인가요?
What do you mostly do when you're on vacation?

주로 여행을 가는데, 나이를 먹으니 가까운 곳으로 ¹호캉스를 가거나 집에 틀어박혀 있는 것도 나쁘지 않더라구요. 요즘 코로나라서 함부로 못 다니니까 더 그렇구요.

16.6 휴가 때 주로 하는 것은 무엇인가요?
What do you mostly do when you're on vacation?

전 사실 엄청난 집순이에 극심한 내향형이여서 방학 되면 대부분의 시간을 집에서 보내요 ㅎㅎ 집에 있으면 영화나 드라마 정주행하면 금방 시간이 지나요. 물론 집에만 있는 거는 아니고 짧게 친구들이나 가족들이랑 여행을 가기도 해요!!

16.7 휴가 때 주로 하는 것은 무엇인가요?
What do you mostly do when you're on vacation?

저는 요즘 ①호캉스 즐겨요! 코로나 전이라면 해외 여행이라고 답변했겠지만, 코로나 이후 ②언텍트 시대가 도래되면서 호텔에 가서 나만의 시간을 여유롭게 가지면서 충전하는게 좋더라구요. 새로운 공간에서 맛있는 음식도 먹으면서 휴식을 취하면 피로도 가시고 충전할 수 있어 좋아요!

¹ 호캉스 - [full: 호텔에서 보내는 호화로운 바캉스] a short vacation at a nearby luxury resort/hotel
² 언텍트 시대 - this period of non-contact; a word originating during covid-19 guidelines

4B 여행

16.8 휴가 때 주로 하는 것은 무엇인가요?
What do you mostly do when you're on vacation?

사실 전 집에 있는 게 최고에요. 침대 밖은 위험합니다. 이불 뒤집어 쓰고 핸드폰이나 노트북 보고 있는 게 진정한 휴가죠. 여행 가는 걸 물어보시는 거면 주로 패키지여행을 다녀서 그냥 버스 타고 관광지 가서 인증사진 찍고 버스 타고 다음 관광지 가고 식당 가고 화장실 가고. 무슨 사육 당하는 거 같아요.

여행 4B

17.01 여긴 정말 꼭 가 봐야 한다는 장소가 있나요? Where is a place you think everyone should visit?

미국이요. 제가 지금 살고 있는 곳이죠. 살면서 미국 한 번은 와 봐야 된다는 생각이 드는 곳입니다.

17.02 여긴 정말 꼭 가 봐야 한다는 장소가 있나요? Where is a place you think everyone should visit?

3년 전에 다낭에 패키지 여행을 갔습니다. 가서 맛난 것도 많이 먹고 경치도 즐겼죠. 현지 길거리 음식을 못 먹어 본 게 아쉽네요.

17.03 여긴 정말 꼭 가 봐야 한다는 장소가 있나요? Where is a place you think everyone should visit?

그런 장소는 개인적으로 없는 것 같습니다. 애초에 한국에 사니까 타지인들에겐 매력적인 장소를 매력적이라고 생각하지 못하는 탓이 큰 것 같네요

17.04 여긴 정말 꼭 가 봐야 한다는 장소가 있나요? Where is a place you think everyone should visit?

오로라는 꼭 보고 싶어요. 제 스마트폰 카메라에서도 잘 찍혀야 페이스북에 올려서 자랑할텐데 말이죠 ㅎㅎ

4B 여행

17.05 여긴 정말 꼭 가 봐야 한다는 장소가 있나요?
Where is a place you think everyone should visit?

장소가 정확하지 않지만 베트남 어시장을 꼭 가봐야 한다고 생각해요. 여행 마지막 만찬을 거기서 즐겼는데, 포켓몬스터의 지우가① 포켓몬을 잡는것 같았어요. 물론 포켓몬 대신 물고기, 포켓볼 대신 내 입.

17.06 여긴 정말 꼭 가 봐야 한다는 장소가 있나요?
Where is a place you think everyone should visit?

저는 강진 완전 추천해요!! 특히 저처럼 유적지 보는 것 좋아하는 사람은 강진은 꼭 한번 가봐야 되요!! 저는 자차로② 이동해서 대중교통이 어떤지는 모르겠지만 정약용 유배지③ 같이 볼만한 곳들이 많고 다 분위기도 좋아서 정말 기억에 남았어요.

17.07 여긴 정말 꼭 가 봐야 한다는 장소가 있나요?
Where is a place you think everyone should visit?

국내에선 대관령 양떼 목장 근처에 소동물 체험관이 있어요! 넓은 부지에 오리, 병아리, 강아지, 말, 양, 낙타 등 여러 동물들을 만져보고 체험할 수 있는 곳이에요. 해외에선 일본 고베쪽에 배를 타고 강 풍류를 즐기는 곳이 있었는데 너무 기억에 남네요.

---

[1] In Korean, "Ash" the Pokemon Trainer's name is 지우
[2] 자차 - [full: 자신의 자동차] meaning "my (personal) car"
[3] 정약용 유배지 - the house where the famous Joseon scholar Jeong Yak-yong was exiled

여행 4B

17.08 여긴 정말 꼭 가 봐야 한다는 장소가 있나요?
Where is a place you think everyone should visit?

한국에서는 아무래도 서울이죠. 수도다 보니까 볼거리 놀거리가 다 밀집되어 있을 수 밖에 없어요ㅋㅋㅋ 저도 맘 편히 놀고 싶을 땐 서울가는 기차표부터 삽니다. 서울이 아니라면 인천이나 부산같은 큰 바다와 항구가 있는 곳들이 은근 재밌습니다. 해외의 경우에는... 제가 해외 여행을 간 경험은 별로 없어서 잘 모르겠네요ㅠㅠ

17.09 여긴 정말 꼭 가 봐야 한다는 장소가 있나요?
Where is a place you think everyone should visit?

로마요! 취직 후 다니던 회사의 본부가 이탈리아 로마에 있어 처음으로 로마로 출장을 가게 되었어요. 말로만 꼭 가봐야할 명소라고 들었던 로마는 실제로 보니 더욱더 아름답고 매력적이었어요. 온 시내를 걸어다니면서 이곳 저곳 숨겨진 유적지 보는게 너무 좋더라구요. 맛있는 음식은 덤이구요! ㅎㅎ

17.10 여긴 정말 꼭 가 봐야 한다는 장소가 있나요?
Where is a place you think everyone should visit?

여러곳을 많이 가본건 아니지만 제가 가본 여행지중에서는 부산이 가장 좋았습니다. 휴가다운 휴가라는 느낌이 들었습니다. 다만 여행의 목적이 전통성을 느끼기 위함이거나 조용한 휴가가 목적이면 비추천드릴게요. 여긴 제2의 서울이거든요 ㅎ 번외로 안 가본중에서는 제주도를 꼭 가보고 싶네요. 주변지인들 말로는 다들 좋았다고 하더라구요 ㅎ

4B 여행

17.11 여긴 정말 꼭 가 봐야 한다는 장소가 있나요?
Where is a place you think everyone should visit?

자본주의 사회에 살고 있는 사람으로써, 서양문화권의 공산주의 국가인 쿠바는 정말 여러모로 흥미로운 나라였습니다.

우선 물질적으로는 풍요롭지 않아도 사람들의 정신적 여유로움 - 혹은 권태에서 오는 느긋함 - 이 처음엔 어색하게 느껴지다가, 급박하고 조급함이 몸에 베어 있던 내게서 차츰 여유로움을 갖게 해주었습니다. 한국에선 별거아닌것이 현지에서는 귀한것이었고, 한국에선 듣도 보도 못한 음식과 과일들이 그들에게는 일상이었습니다. 어느 나라나 비슷한 문화권이 아니라면 거기에서 오는 이질감이 있기 마련이나, 제게는 그 이질감이 위화감이 아닌 신선함으로 다가왔습니다. 글자 그대로 저녁이 있는 삶을① 살고 있는 사람들이었습니다.

흔히들 쿠바를 시간이 멈춘 나라라고 하지만, 최근에는 인터넷도 보급되면서 젊은이들을 중심으로 빠르게 변화 하고 있습니다.

저는 음주를 좋아합니다. 쿠바의 대표적인 술이 럼 인데 럼은 사탕수수를 발효해서 만든 술입니다. 발효된 사탕수수를 증류하고 숙성하여 만든는데 저는 '아바나 끌룹' 7년산을 럼중에서 가장 좋아합니다. 말레꼰에 앉아서 밤바람을 맞으며 마셨던 '아바나 끌룹'은 아직도 잊혀지지 않습니다. 기회가 된다면 꼭 쿠바에 가보는것 을 추천합니다.

---

[1] 저녁이 있는 삶 - (lit. "a life with dinners") - Most Korean people work very late and are unable to enjoy meals with family or friends. A lifestyle where people can do this regularly seems novel.

여행 4B

18.01 현지 언어를 할 줄 모르는 곳을 여행해 본 적이 있나요? 어땠나요? Have you ever travelled somewhere where [...]

일본을 갔는데 말이 통하지는 않았지만 사람들이 친절해서 잘 도와줘서 좋았어요.

18.02 현지 언어를 할 줄 모르는 곳을 여행해 본 적이 있나요? 어땠나요? Have you ever travelled somewhere where [...]

스페인어를 모르는 상태에서 1년 간 남미여행을 갔습니다. "맛있다", "얼마예요?" 등 간단한 문장, 숫자들만 현지에서 익히고 재미있게 다녔습니다.

18.03 현지 언어를 할 줄 모르는 곳을 여행해 본 적이 있나요? 어땠나요? Have you ever travelled somewhere where [...]

아쉽지만 해외여행경험이 없어요. 기회만 된다면 동남아, 미국, 유럽 등등 많은 곳을 경험해 보고싶네요. 특히 동남아의 그 달디달다[1] 과일이 너무 궁금합니다!

18.04 현지 언어를 할 줄 모르는 곳을 여행해 본 적이 있나요? 어땠나요? Have you ever travelled somewhere where [...]

제가 여행했던 곳은 전부 영어권이 아니어서 제가 말이 잘 통하지는 않았는데, 바디 랭귀지를 하면 어느 정도 통하더라고요.

[1] 달디달다 is a technically incorrect (yet widely used and accepted) spelling of 다디달다, meaning very sweet, or super sweet.

4B 여행

18.05 현지 언어를 할 줄 모르는 곳을 여행해 본 적이 있나요? 어땠나요? Have you ever travelled somewhere where you didn't speak the language? How did it go?

태국 가봤습니다. 간단한 영어로도 어느정도는 소통이 가능해서 현지어를 몰라도 큰 지장은 없었습니다. 음식이 맛있어서 좋았구요. 날씨가 엄청 덥긴 했으나 그정도는 예상하고 갔던터라 별 문제 없었습니다. 다만 카드 결제가 안될 때가 있어서 약간 불편했습니다.

18.06 현지 언어를 할 줄 모르는 곳을 여행해 본 적이 있나요? 어땠나요? Have you ever travelled somewhere where you didn't speak the language? How did it go?

제가 이모와 함께 간 북한의 신의주시입니다. 표준어와는 거리가 좀 멀기는 하였으나 제가 학창시절 배웠던 북한말을 잘 알고 있어서 다행히 북한으로 넘어오는데 크게 지장은 없었고 심지어 이모는 북한에서 살다 오신 분이셔서 여느 때보다 순조롭게 여행할 수 있었습니다.

18.07 현지 언어를 할 줄 모르는 곳을 여행해 본 적이 있나요? 어땠나요? Have you ever travelled somewhere where you didn't speak the language? How did it go?

현지 언어를 할 줄 모르는 곳으로 여행을 떠난 적이 있었습니다. 여행 가기 전 까지는 걱정과 우려가 있었지만, 막상 여행을 떠나고 맞부딪쳐보고 나니 재미있고 즐거운 시간들을 경험하게 되었습니다. 여행을 더 즐겁고 유익하게 보내기 위해 최대한 영어를 사용하는 것을 자제하였습니다.

여행 4B

18.08 현지 언어를 할 줄 모르는 곳을 여행해 본 적이 있나요? 어땠나요? Have you ever travelled somewhere where you didn't speak the language? How did it go?

베트남에 갔었어요. 대책없이 인삿말도 모르는 채로 다녔는데 웬걸! 지금 한국인지 베트남인지도 모를만큼 한국어를 다 쓰시던데요.. ㅋㅋㅋ 그렇지 않은 곳도 간단한 영어와 바디랭귀지로 다 통했습니다.

18.09 현지 언어를 할 줄 모르는 곳을 여행해 본 적이 있나요? 어땠나요? Have you ever travelled somewhere where you didn't speak the language? How did it go?

저번에 일본 오키나와에 갔었는데 가이드가 있어서 괜찮았지만 혼자 편의점에갔을때 직원분들의 말을 못알아들어서 당황했던 기억이 있네요. ㅎㅎ 저는 그런 해프닝때문에 여행이 다 재미있었던거 같아요.

18.10 현지 언어를 할 줄 모르는 곳을 여행해 본 적이 있나요? 어땠나요? Have you ever travelled somewhere where you didn't speak the language? How did it go?

[1] 노랑풍선과 함께 캄보디아와 중국 여행을 갔습니다. 둘다 훌륭한 가이드 덕분에 큰 문제는 없었지만 길거리 상인들과 거래가 매우 힘들었습니다. 언어 소통에 문제가 있어 만원 정도 삥 뜯긴걸로 알고 있어요 ㅎㅎㅎ.

---

[1] 노랑풍선 (YellowBalloon) is a Korean-based company engaged in provision of travel industry.

4B 여행

19.01 가장 별로였던 휴가는 언제인가요? 어떤일이 있었나요? What is your worst vacation memory?

장마 때 캠핑을 갔는데 비가 넘쳐서 텐트가 강물에 떠내려 갔어요.

19.02 가장 별로였던 휴가는 언제인가요? 어떤일이 있었나요? What is your worst vacation memory?

전주로 여행을 간 적이 있는데 정말 끔찍했습니다. 한옥에 별의별 간판들을 다 메달아 놔서 예쁘지도 않고 밥은 또 얼마나 비싸던지 정말 비추합니다.

19.03 가장 별로였던 휴가는 언제인가요? 어떤일이 있었나요? What is your worst vacation memory?

여친과 같이 여행을 갔는데 가서 대판 싸워서 서로 씩씩대고 호텔에서 하루종일 그냥 있었을때가 생각나네요 ㅠㅠ

19.04 가장 별로였던 휴가는 언제인가요? 어떤일이 있었나요? What is your worst vacation memory?

베트남은 갈때마다 바가지를 씁니다. 화폐단위가 커서 계산하기도 힘들고 베트남 상인들은 항상 여행객을 뜯어먹으려고 합니다. 물론 음식은 맛있어서 자주 갑니다

여행 4B

19.05 가장 별로였던 휴가는 언제인가요? 어떤일이 있었나요?
What is your worst vacation memory?

즉흥적으로 휴가철을 보내려고 하다가 결국 아무것도 안하고 집에서 누우면서 넷플릭스만 봤던 적이 있었습니다. 이 이후로 왠만하면 휴가철 때 계획을 잡고 조금 더 유익하게 보내려고 하고 있습니다.

19.06 가장 별로였던 휴가는 언제인가요? 어떤일이 있었나요?
What is your worst vacation memory?

겨울에 대천에 갔을때요. 17시간 가까이 무수면+공복 상태에 찬바람을 맞으며 걷다 남자친구와 싸움... 근무때문에 밤샘해서 매우 멍한 상태에 계속 걷기만 하고 쉬지 못해서 신경질이 나서 결국엔 폭발했음.

19.07 가장 별로였던 휴가는 언제인가요? 어떤일이 있었나요?
What is your worst vacation memory?

4월 쯔음에 호캉스를 다녀왔는데, 학생인 아는 동생이랑 다녀왔어요. 제가 훨씬 더 많은 돈을 내고 다녀온 건데, 아무런 계획 없이 간 거라서 너무 심심했어요. 다음엔 영화라도 노트북에 담아와야겠어요.. ㅎㅎㅎ

4B 여행

19.08 가장 별로였던 휴가는 언제인가요? 어떤일이 있었나요? What is your worst vacation memory?

가는길에 차가 막혀 멀미도 하고 가서 아파서 구경도 제대로 못하고 차에만 있었던적이 있었는데 너무 어릴때라서 몇살때였는지는 기억나지 않습니다.

19.09 가장 별로였던 휴가는 언제인가요? 어떤일이 있었나요? What is your worst vacation memory?

근 3~4년간 너무 바쁘고 우울해서 휴가라면 다 좋았습니다. 하지만 2년 전 송도에 놀러갔을 때 하루종일 비가 와서 그건 좀 아쉬웠네요.

19.10 가장 별로였던 휴가는 언제인가요? 어떤일이 있었나요? What is your worst vacation memory?

저는 일본 도쿄 갔을 때가 제일 별로 였던 것 같아요. 일단 그때 먹었던 음식이 다 안 맞아서 도쿄에 있던 동안 호텔 조식만 먹고 거의 굶었어요 ㅠㅠ. (이상하게도 오사카 갔을 때는 너무 잘 먹었다는 사실.... 아마 계속 식당을 잘못 고른 거 같아요 ㅠㅠ) 그리고 디즈니 랜드 가서도 재미없는 놀이기구 타느라 퍼레이드도 놓쳤고요. 게다가 같이 갔던 아는 동생이 자꾸 칭얼대서 빨리 호텔로 가야 해서 너무 아쉬웠어요.

여행 4B

20.1 일등석이나 비지니스석을 타 본 적이 있나요? Have you ever travelled in first class or business class?

가난한 여행자라 탄적은 없습니다. 경유를 하더라도 가장 저렴한 티켓을 끊어서 여행다닙니다.

20.2 일등석이나 비지니스석을 타 본 적이 있나요? Have you ever travelled in first class or business class?

아뇨 비행기자체를 타본적이 없어요.. 꼭 나중에 부모님 모시고 일등석은 무리일지 몰라도 비지니스석으로 여행가보고 싶어요. ㅎ

20.3 일등석이나 비지니스석을 타 본 적이 있나요? Have you ever travelled in first class or business class?

저희 아빠는 파일럿이에요! 그래서 어렸을때부터 비행기를 많이 탔답니다. 일등석을 타본건 손에 꼽을 정도지만 비즈니스석은 많이 타봤어요.

20.4 일등석이나 비지니스석을 타 본 적이 있나요? Have you ever travelled in first class or business class?

한번 타보고는 싶네요... 주로 여행은 배낭여행 스타일로 가서 비행기 탈 때도 일반 좌석에 앉아서 갔어요.

4B 여행

20.5 일등석이나 비지니스석을 타 본 적이 있나요?
Have you ever travelled in first class or business class?

아니요! 돈을 많이 벌게 되면 한 번쯤은 타보고 싶긴 하네요. 제가 주로 갔던 외국은 중국 아니면 일본이라 인천국제공항에서 1~2시간이면 충분히 가거든요. 비싼 돈 주고 산 좌석을 얼마 쓰지도 못한다면 돈이 아깝잖아요^^;

20.6 일등석이나 비지니스석을 타 본 적이 있나요?
Have you ever travelled in first class or business class?

네 자주 타봤어요. 일등석에서 계속 포도랑 치즈를 시켰더니 스튜어디스가 다른분도 먹어야 한다면서 안줄때까지 시켜봐서 진상고객도 되봤어요. 코리안에어를 타면 일등석 뒤에 바도 있어서 무료칵테일들도 만들어줘요. 근데 전 금주 중이라 못먹어서 아깝더래요.

20.7 일등석이나 비지니스석을 타 본 적이 있나요?
Have you ever travelled in first class or business class?

남편이랑 4개월간 프랑스에 갈일이있었어요. 워낙 긴 비행 시간이라 비즈니스로 업그레이드 해서 항공권을 끊었어요. 둘다 짧은 구간만 비즈니스로 탄지라, 제대로 비즈니스칸을 구경해 본적이 없었는데 이번에는 제대로 할수 있었죠. 무료 바도있고, 식사는 코스로 나오고 신기한거 투성이었어요! 다리도 쭉피고 잘수 있어서 아주 편안하게 다녀올수 있었답니다.

여행 4B

NOTES

4B 여행

NOTES

05 번역

TRANSLATIONS

05 번역

경험

1. Have you ever won a contest?

1.1 When I was young, I attended a drawing contest organized by Lotte at my kindergarten. I tried to just draw part of the corner of a building, and even that I couldn't draw well so I wasn't expecting anything, but they said my drawing was really creative, so I remember winning second place. I also remember winning an enormous teddy bear.

1.2 Yes! I won a gold medal in a philosophy writing contest. I didn't think I would win the gold medal - when I was on the list I was so surprised! I think the philosophy writing subject was 'The Duty of the Nation'. It was a difficult subject, so I wasn't expecting to get a good result, but surprisingly I won, so I was really happy.

1.3 I haven't been in many contests, but in high school I won the grand prize in political writing. The president at the time was Geun-hye Park, and I wrote nearly 3,000 characters worth of harsh criticisms on the problems and planned policies of the government at that time.

1.4 When I was young I played piano. While attending a piano class with my friends, I went to a domestic competition and won an award. It's not easy to put so much time and effort into one song and then be evaluated in a moment. It was so stressful waiting for my turn. But since I went to the concert with my friends I could keep a clear head while I waited. I'm thankful to my teacher and my friends for helping me.

1.5 Yes. It was last fall. The Gyeongsangbuk-do Office of Education held a youth hackathon (I don't remember the official name), and it was a contest where three or four people form a team to make and present a computer program within two days. About thirty-five teams attended the preliminaries and seven teams made it to the finals. So we made the program (the program our team made was to help independent study) and presented it. The results came out thirty minutes to an hour later and our team won first place.

1.6 I won an English drama competition when I was in elementary school. My friends and I performed Beauty and the Beast and I was the fairy who cast a spell on the Beast. I didn't have many lines, but I felt the pressure because they were in English. So I practiced my lines dozens of times and practiced in the mirror. And after school, my friends and I would meet up and try to work on it together. Finally the day of the presentation arrived and I performed my part without making any mistakes. When the judge called our name first, we were so happy that we screamed and cheered together. It was a very rewarding and happy moment.

2. Have you ever been somewhere haunted? If so, where was it?

2.1 Yes, I was passing through the first floor basement of Acrovista at night (which is the site of the Sampoong Department Store collapse in 1995), when I saw something far away with the shape of a person wearing white clothes (I don't remember the details). Five minutes later when I went back they were gone.

2.2 Well, if you go at night to the old battlegrounds from the Korean War in 1950, ghosts of old Chinese or North Korean soldiers might appear. Of course, I hear there are also locations haunted by the ghosts of Korean or UN forces, too.

2.3 I've never been somewhere actually haunted, but when I was young I went to a haunted house at an amusement park. They weren't real ghosts, just people dressed up as ghosts, so I wasn't afraid, but I'd get startled when they'd suddenly jump out of the dark spaces.

2.4 I haven't been anywhere haunted, but there are some places where I think I heard a ghost. A few years ago, when my boyfriend lived with his parents, I went over to his place and his room was inthe basement. We were having fun hanging out in his room watching a movie, when suddenly the newton's cradle in the cabinet above the TV started the pendulum movement according to the law of energy conservation. It's funny to say this, but after that day, toys up on the shelf would occasionally move or fall off, so I remember getting goosebumps.

2.5 Haunted places… I haven't been. Haha. Um, but still, sometimes when I come home at dawn I'm a little scared of riding the elevator at my apartment. Of course, the lights are on, it's a big apartment complex so there's lots of buildings, and there's lots of people living there - if something happened, everyone would come and check it out, so it's not like there's much to be afraid of but.. still.. Haha. It's scary, you know? Lol. Just me being me~

2.6 Yup! I'm not a person who gets scared easily. Haha. I went to an abandoned house, though I don't believe in ghosts so I wasn't scared. But I think the people who were afraid of ghosts (and the creepy atmosphere) hated it.

2.7 I've never gone looking for ghosts. But I heard that our barracks in the army were haunted, so it seems like I might've lived with one I guess.

2.8 I tend to believe in ghosts and psychics, so I purposely never go to places like that because I worry that, on the off chance, something bad could happen.

2.9 I get traumatized when I watch horror movies, so I never watch them. I'm really curious about haunted places, but I tend to block out information about them.

3. Do you go to the market? If so, what do you usually buy there?

3.1 I don't really go to the market. But if there's one food I have to buy at the market - it's rice cakes (tteok). Especially mugwort rice cakes (ssuk tteok). The bigger the market and the bigger the shop, the more delicious varieties there'll be. You definitely have to try it~

3.2 I mostly go to Costco. I usually start shopping by making a list of all the items I need for the week, but in the end I tend to impulsively buy things that I don't end up eating or using!

3.3 I usually go to big supermarkets to shop. But I've been with my mother in the past. She still shops at the market. She buys the vegetables that the old ladies grow by hand, or the vegetables picked on the mountains. At the market she also often buys seafood, like fish and shellfish, rice cakes made at the mill, and flour. There's lots of cheap and delicious foods at the market. When I went with her to shop, we would buy and eat guksu or sujaebi (noodle soups). To me, the market is a place that reminds me of my mom.

3.4 I originally loved going to the market. The sounds of the merchant's voices and the unique atmosphere makes the market feel alive. So when I was young, whenever I was stressed about something, or when I was bored, I went to the market to look around. But lately, because I've moved, there is no market nearby so I'm only going to the supermarket :'(

3.5 I live in the countryside so I go to the neighborhood supermarket or to the country market when it opens. The country market is called 'The Five Day Market,' so being a market that opens on every 5th day, in our neighborhood it opens on every day that ends in a 2 or a 7. If you go to the market, you can buy things cheaper and fresher than the regular stores, and street vendors come so you can also buy good snacks.

3.6 No, I don't. The neighborhood where I live is a new planned development, so there's no market. Sometimes on holidays I go to my grandmother's house, and then we go to the market! Because we need to buy the ingredients to prepare the memorial services. At the market near my grandmother's house I buy fruit, fish, and other things to eat like rice cakes (tteok).

3.7 As for markets, I tend to go to the fish markets a lot. I live in Incheon so there are big fish markets like Sorae Port and Yeonan Pier. Also if there's a special occasion or if I want to make a special dinner, I go to the fish market that day to buy fresh seafood. Since the west sea is famous for blue crab, in the spring I buy blue crabs with roe, and make soy sauce marinated crab or spicy marinated crab. In the fall, I buy the male crabs that have gotten big and fat and eat steamed crab.

4. Have you ever done military service? If so, what was your experience like?

4.01 Yes, I served in the navy for twenty-eight months and if I could just forget the experience as much as possible that would be nice.

4.02 Yes. It was really not great. I was able to enjoy the feeling of having my freedom stolen away. I don't want to go back.

4.03 Yes I've done my military duty. If I were to describe my experience, even a week of talking wouldn't be enough, but if I were to sum it up in one sentence: it was shit.

4.04 If you're a healthy man in Korea, you've experienced it. 'Cause we're conscripted. When I enlisted I felt like I was gonna die, but after I got out of the army, I felt pretty good about myself and I think I lived like a real macho man for a while. Haha

4.05 I've never done military service. In Korea, only men are obligated to serve, and women don't have a duty to do so. Only the type of women who want to become professional soldiers do military service. So a woman like me has never gone to the military.

4.06 I'm scheduled to do military service around the end of next year. My friends in my year group have already joined and are living that military life. I'm so sad. Won't I be marching in the army by the time this book comes out? Haha.

4.07 I haven't joined the army yet, but I'll have to soon. The Korean army is conscripted, so the men have to do military service no matter what. The thought of having to go to the army is really stressing me out these days. It's stressful being closed off in the military when we're in our twenties - in our prime. In addition, the Korean military doesn't give the soldiers a minimum wage. I think the military is the place that gives the least amount of consideration to a person.

4.08 There was such a hodgepodge of people since all different people came from all different regions. Even though we weren't close, there were some people that were so memorable that I still remember their names even though it's been twenty years. Shooting was the most fun. Even though I was in a comfortable unit, every year for fifteen years after I was discharged, I had nightmares about going back. But now the 'Warrior Platform' project is underway, and after thinking about getting to touch all that equipment - I haven't had a nightmare about re-enlistment since.

4.09 Yup! I'm a Korean man so basically all of us go, right? I joined the army in a special position called a Katusa. A Katusa is an abbreviation for the Korean Augmentation to the US Army!! I haven't been to the USA but the life I had in the US army was SO good. My military life might have been comfortable, but when I trained or worked, I worked harder than anyone else. Just in case I could represent Koreans well to others in the army. Still to this day, my time in the military is the memory that has left the greatest impression on my life.

191

4.10 I haven't done military service, but my older brother worked in the army for two years, and my uncle served as a colonel in the marines. My older brother said it was a good experience but he doesn't want to go back.

4.11 Yes. I joined the army on November 18th, 2019, and I was discharged on June 3rd, 2021. I spent my military life in Cheorwon, in the Gangwon region, which is known as Korea's 'Siberia'. If we're talking interesting experiences, it snows a lot in Gangwon, so even though we should have been resting on the weekends, I have lots of memories of snow piling up and clearing it out. Also, I remember secretly eating ramen in the evenings with my military brothers in the mess hall without the senior officers knowing. As for a proud experience, one time after a training exercise I remember doing what I could to finish successfully. But there were bad experiences, too. While doing my training, a senior officer accidentally cut my upper arm and it left a scar. The officer didn't apologize, so that left a bad memory. If you ask me overall what my experience in the military was like, I would say "If I have the same brothers in arms, I could do it again."

5. Have you ever had something stolen?

5.1 Yes. When I was young we lived in an apartment on the first floor. I was out with my mom and my younger sibling, and when we came back the house was a mess. A burglar had broken in. My piggy bank, that I had been putting all my allowance money in since I was born, was stolen. If you counted it up, there was probably KRW$1,000,000 (about $900 USD) in there...

5.2 When I was young a friend came over to my house to play and I showed him my expensive gameboy… then it disappeared and I cried so much. And then a few weeks later my friend replaced the one I lost, but no matter how I think about it, that wasn't something they bought - that was mine. I don't even remember talking to him after that.

5.3 In the past in fifth grade (when I was twelve?). It was a rainy day. The hagwon I went to had a place to put umbrellas right in front of the entrance doors. I put the red umbrella I came with there, right? But when the hagwon ended and I was going home, my umbrella was gone. I haven't seen that umbrella since.

5.4 Um…. only once. In my high school days, one of my mechanical pencils disappeared. I didn't lose it - I thought to myself "looks like somebody stole it", so for a few days I carefully observed what the other students were carrying. After three days one of my classmates was rummaging in their bag and out came my mechanical pencil! As soon as I saw it I said it was mine and asked them why they had taken it, and they got all awkward. I got so mad and took it back.

5.5 I have had something stolen. I gave this box of cigarettes that had been flown in from North Korea to my friend as a birthday present. At some point I realized I didn't see the cigarettes. The friend I gave the present to was my roommate, and I hadn't seen him smoking them - from some point on I just never saw them. We all thought it was really weird. But then, we went to a different friend's house and the cigarettes were there. It was so ridiculous and I was totally shook.

5.6 It wasn't anything expensive, but I once had a reading lamp stolen at school. The school I went to was a boarding school, so we had to study until 11pm every day. The spot where I studied had dim lighting so I definitely needed a reading lamp. So I used to bring a small reading lamp from home to study with, and one day it was just stolen? It was totally ridiculous.

5.7 I haven't had anything stolen, but I did get burned doing something against my better judgment. This happened over ten years ago, but when I was young my parents gave me a watch for kids and my friend who went to the same daycare as me said he wanted to try it on, so I let him borrow it, and then the next day, while saying my watch was something his parents had given him, he told me not to covet other people's things. Should I count this as theft? This is the only story I have to tell about having something taken or stolen from me in my life. I was really burned by this huge betrayal - I even got really sensitive about my belongings, though I think I'm less likely to lose my things because of that experience.

능력

6. Are you good at handling electronics and machines?

6.1 No. I'm not good at handling machines, and looking at the machine manuals is always annoying.

6.2 It depends on the machine. I don't object to it any more than other women do. I've been messing around with this and that by myself ever since I was young.

6.3 I like handling machines. Most of the parts on my motorcycle I've replaced myself. The engine oil, brake lining, tyres, etc.

6.4 I can use simple machines without an instruction manual. Even with complex machines, it's possible for me to use them with just the instruction manual. Of course, things to do with the core components or any kind of repairs are out of the question.

6.5 I'm pretty good with them. I have an older sister and while she's technologically challenged, I'm good with things here and there, so I always seem to have to fix stuff at home or handle machine related stuff.

6.6 Yes, I'm pretty good with them. I've enjoyed messing with machinery ever since I was young. So now, for the most part, if something breaks down or doesn't work right, I can fix it and reassemble it with ease.

6.7 I'm not good with all machines. But to some extent, for things that I use in my daily life I can get by if there's at least an instruction manual. For example, I can simply replace batteries, or assemble things, but I'm not good at finding problems and fixing things on machines I've never seen before. Actually, I can learn how to do it on Youtube and various media, but in my case, when I'm learning to handle new machines, I would much rather meet somebody and learn how to do it from them directly. Of course, I'm saying all this, but in fact, I'm somebody who's often heard that I'm tech illiterate.

6.8 I'm 'technologically challenged'. When I was young my younger sibling was really good with new devices and machines, and now they're employed and working at Samsung Electronics. But I'm not like that; when I buy new devices, even if I refer to the user manual, it's so complicated for me that I have to figure it out through the internet (youtube videos). I'm always jealous of people who are good with machines and know how to use them.

7. Can you speak another language?

7.1 I can speak English and Japanese. English I learned in school from middle school onwards, and I like Japanese culture so I am currently learning it via self study.

7.2 Yes, I can speak English. I think when it comes to foreign languages, almost all Koreans speak English the best. Since Korean students learn it all through school. The unfortunate thing is that we're learning English for the college entrance exams, so we just learn English to pass tests rather than for speaking.

7.3 Yes, I can speak English. I tend to have casual conversations no problem. But there are times where I can't understand because of the other person's pronunciation or speed, and sometimes when they use words or idioms I don't know, I can understand, but it's difficult. And I've also studied Japanese and German, but outside of simple expressions I'm not very good.

7.4 I know how to speak English and a little bit of Japanese. And I think I can copy foreign accents pretty well. So even though I only know a few words, my accent misleads people to think I'm much better at the language than I actually am. Even though I can really only use the Japanese I know to a certain extent. But when I go to Japan and speak with local people, they think I'm really good at Japanese and give me really long answers. But of course I can only reply "I... I'm sorry..."

7.5 In high school I learned Japanese, and I was pretty good at it, but now I can only really introduce myself by name. Because I'm currently living in America I'm learning and using English. I'm experiencing first-hand that learning a language is much harder than I thought it would be. I work and look after the kids so learning a language is harder than I thought. I tend to say only what I need to say. Even so, as time goes by, even if it's just a little at a time, I think, 'surely I'll get better?'

8. Is it easy for you to get along with people?

8.1 I kind of think it is and I kind of think it isn't. I think it gets easier for us to get along with others when we become adults.

8.2 Yes, I tend to. Though as I get older there are fewer opportunities to meet new people, and I don't really try to meet new people either.

8.3 I don't think so. I think it takes a while to get along with other people. I can make small talk with people I meet for the first time, but it's not really that comfortable for me. I think it's hard to know what to talk about. It's okay if we have things in common, or we get along well, but it's kinda hard getting along with people who I don't have much in common with. When I was young I could make friends without even thinking about it, but I think it's gotten more difficult as I've gotten older. Sometimes it seems sad but on the other hand I think it's just the natural way of things.

8.4 Yes. I usually get along with people easily. I do various hobbies, so I talk a lot more and get along more easily with the other person, especially when they enjoy those same hobbies. I enjoy motorbikes, kayaking, billiards, swimming, golf, and fishing.

8.5 I usually get along with others right away. Since I can't stand an awkward atmosphere. I lead the conversation first. But I think it takes a long time to build a deep relationship. I guess I don't trust other people easily. Haha.

8.6 Yes, I get along with people pretty well. The people I'm close to tend to be diverse in age. I'm the kind of person that approaches others with ease. However, I don't get close with just anyone, nor do I set out first thing to get close with somebody. But at least, when I meet people in a natural setting, in a professional setting, or for whatever other reasons, I can approach them without difficulty.

8.7 I tend to get close to other people pretty easily. Personally, I think manners are important in interpersonal relationships, so it's easier for me to get close to people who can feel the weight of their words, expressions, actions, etc. I totally agree with the old proverb "One word can repay a thousand nyang debt." Words show a person's social background and class, so I think one can maintain a healthy relationship with polite and well-mannered people.

8.8 The degree of closeness and meaning of being close might be different for different people, but I think I have an affinity for meeting somebody for the first time and establishing a good relationship with them. So when I meet somebody I can easily open up and get close to them. But I need time to develop a deeper relationship. As I get to know somebody, if our beliefs and values are different, I can't really develop a deep relationship with them, but I don't think it's uncomfortable to make small talk. Actually as you get older, it's not easy to find true friends, but I'm good at putting myself out there, so that's why I can say I make friends easily. Well, but I guess I don't know about the other person... Ha.

9. Do you tend to stick to your commitments?

9.1 Yes I tend to. I'm especially sensitive about time commitments. So I get pretty stressed. But there is one commitment I can't stick to very well: and that's my diet commitments.

9.2 Yes I tend to keep my promises. I don't like to be late so I leave early but... although I don't intend to be, I've been late these days because I recently started driving and I'm not very good. Haha. But if I am late, I text or call first to let the other person know.

9.3 Yes, I tend to keep my word. It's a given that you should keep to important promises at all costs, right? Above all I make an effort to keep promises to family or close friends. I think it might be because I'm aware that we perceive people who don't keep their promises to be unreliable. Be that as it may, I'm not always a perfect person who keeps all their promises.

9.4 Yes, I stick to my word. I never leave late, and I prepare my work in advance, although sometimes there are variables like traffic jams or illness.

9.5 Sometimes there are circumstances where I can't keep a promise because I don't remember or due to some unavoidable reason. And I'm a person who doesn't like to make promises I can't keep.

9.6 I do when it comes to work. After all, if there's a strict deadline, I think the process has to follow it anyway. The same goes for my promises to other people. But there are situations where I postpone or cancel my appointments. For situations out of my control, or for illness, at least the day before, I talk with the other person and figure out some other arrangement. And for the day of the appointment, if there's nothing special going on, I leave a little quicker or set a time. Because if I do that, it sets my mind at ease.

10. Are you good at expressing how you feel?

10.1 I'm not really that good at expressing how I feel. I tend to think about the other person's position first.

10.2 Yes, I tend to express how I feel honestly, but sometimes I take some time to express my emotions because I need to figure them out first. Especially when I'm angry or disappointed.

10.3 I think it depends on the person. I myself find that I feel secure talking with groups that make me feel safe or with my friends. But! When talking with my work colleagues, people I know through work, even my family, my parents - I don't really express how I feel honestly. For example, I share good feelings and positive things with my parents, but I don't share hard and difficult negative emotions. The reason is I think they'll worry about it. So I have a tendency to always make it look like I'm doing fine.

10.4 When I was young I expressed how I felt honestly. But as I got older and started a social life, from then I discovered it's not a good thing to express my 'feelings' so openly, and so I avoided or refrained from expressing my emotions to close acquaintances and other people outside my family members.

10.1 No. When I was young I would, but now that I'm already in my thirties I don't think I can talk about my feelings with just anyone. Moreover, because I've been hurt expressing myself honestly, I worry about it a lot more, so I

번역 05

think I've naturally become like this.

10.2 No. When I was a little younger I think I did, but becoming careful about expressing how you honestly feel is a part of getting older. Also, I can express both positive and negative emotions to my family openly, but to people outside of my family, save for positive emotions, I don't think there's many times when I talk about negative emotions.

10.3 No. I tend to think that the more I reveal my emotions, the more I reveal my weaknesses, so I tend not to reveal everything.

10.4 Yes. I think I'm really not good at hiding how I feel. I think that could be a strength or a weakness. But the good thing is that my field of work has a lot of freedom so I get less stressed than other regular office workers.

10.5 I think it depends on the situation. I usually express my feelings pretty honestly to my family and close friends. But sometimes the closer I am to somebody, the more I'd rather hide my feelings. Because I'm worried that they might get hurt by what I have to say. So I really try to control my emotions. Rather than suppressing them, I try my best to control how I express myself. I'm the type who tries not to make the situation or the other person uncomfortable with my feelings.

습관

11. What chore do you most hate doing?

11.01 I hate washing dishes the most. Cooking and eating tasty food is all well and good but the sink is so low that it hurts my back. Also, water from the low sink splashes on my clothes and after washing the dishes I have to go get changed.

11.02 There's nothing I especially hate, but there are times when general house cleaning is a pain. Cleaning the windows, cleaning the rugs and carpet, sweeping under the furniture, etc. takes a long time, so I put it off because I don't really want to do it.

11.03 I tend to buy lots of random things so I most dislike organizing! I used to do it once a week but it's hard work every time.

11.04 Washing dishes. I have to stand in one place, and I worry about breaking the dishes, so I get stressed out having to be so cautious.

11.05 Washing dishes is such a pain… Everything about it annoys me. Usually when I wash dishes I don't wear an apron so there're many times when water splashes on my clothes and gets me all wet and it's really annoying. But what can I do… if I don't wash the dishes I'll be in trouble later when I need plates.

11.06 I just dislike household chores themselves haha… I especially hate vacuuming. Ever since I was young I've caught my foot on the vacuum and the cord so many times… I haven't been badly hurt or anything, but you feel my pain right?? Haha

11.07 Actually, I hate all household chores, but I hate folding laundry the most. Whether I'm sitting, standing, or even lying down, my back hurts so bad, I don't even know what I'm doing, and putting the folded laundry away in the dresser is such a pain. Actually doing the laundry is better, but I really hate folding it afterwards.

11.08 I also hate washing dishes. If I put it off till later I hate doing it even more, so as I'm cooking I tend to wash the dishes I use straight away.

11.09 Hanging up the laundry. The nagging I constantly heard from my mom was, "hang up the laundry." So that's why I try to avoid hanging it up. I'm like this even though It's not that hard and it'll only take a minute to finish.

11.10 I'm least confident about cleaning my room. I don't hate it but it's hard to see the difference between before I've cleaned and after, and it's clean by my standards, but others often think it hasn't been cleaned yet. Compared to that, I like doing laundry, bathroom cleaning, and washing the dishes where I can see the results right away.

12. What do you do to start your day?

12.01 In the morning I get up feeling like I just really don't want to...

12.02 Washing my hair! It wakes me up and puts me in the mood to start the day.

12.03 In the morning as soon as I wake up, I always immediately make the bed. I neatly organize the pillows and blankets.

12.04 Before getting out of bed, I start my day by sending my boyfriend a good morning text.

12.05 I lie in bed for an hour and play on my phone... I should probably fix that.

12.06 A glass of water. I heard it's good for your health, and actually it wakes me up a bit.

12.07 When I wake up, I brush my teeth, and after washing my face I drink water. I rarely eat a full (Korean style) breakfast, but sometimes I eat cereal or bread instead. And then I get dressed and go to work right away.

12.08 I eat breakfast. I eat protein-oriented meals on days I work out. Otherwise, I eat low-calorie food.

12.09 In the morning I start my day by going for a walk along the river near my house. I feel refreshed and revived when I drink in the morning air.

12.10 Looking at my phone! I first check KakaoTalk, webtoons, community forums, and notifications from my professors, etc.

12.11 I always start my day by having a shower. I have to go to school, but if I don't immediately have a shower, then I just fall back asleep. So there have been times where I haven't gone to class.

12.12 Usually, I start my day by eating breakfast. I toast bread in the toaster and spread it with my own homemade orange jam, and then I heat up water to drink green tea.

13. How do you find good ideas when working on an important project?

13.01 I jot down ideas that come to me while I'm spacing out and pick from those.

13.02 When I paint I often look through my past material, such as old travel photos and my favorite color combinations.

13.03 I get ideas while discussing with other project members, or I look for whether papers have been conducted on similar topics.

13.04 I think I usually do a lot of brainstorming. After making a lot of ideas like that, I organize them.

13.05 While continuing to talk about related topics, if there's something that looks good I'll write it down. But I think almost all ideas come from within your range of knowledge. I usually read a lot of books and try to make a habit of continually learning from other fields of knowledge.

13.06 I look on the internet. Especially through Naver. The internet is a place that contains all the world's information, both good and bad, so whenever there's something I don't know, I unconsciously end up pulling out my smartphone.

13.07 I usually get ideas from my imagination. Many times the best ideas will come to me when I'm not thinking about my work at all, so ideas often pop up when I'm looking out the window or having a shower.

13.08 I tend to dig up ideas from my daily life. My job is to get people to empathize, so in order to elicit that empathy I need to get ideas from small events or stories that anyone could go through and apply them to my projects.

13.09 First, I search through my own experiences. If my memories are empty or faded, I look for past materials. If I still can't find an answer, I consult my seniors or people I think might know the solution. Because there aren't that many completely new things in the world, right?

13.10 When squeezing out ideas rather than pushing my brain to think about a whole bunch of things, I take some time to think deeply about the first few things that come to mind. I take a short break or purposely work on something else so that my thoughts don't get pulled in any one direction.

14. Are you superstitious? Is there anything you do to avoid 'jinxes' on important days?

14.01 I'm not superstitious. So I don't have any jinxes. On important days I just brace myself and try my best to have a good day.

14.02 I'm not superstitious, but if there is an important day, I tend to wash thoroughly the day before. I take a bath too, if I can.

14.03 I'm not superstitious and I don't have any particular jinxes, but there is a saying that one should not eat seaweed soup before an important exam, so I don't do that.

14.04 I don't tend to be superstitious, and I don't have any jinxes on important days, but sometimes, early in the morning, when things like glass, mirrors, or ceramic cups break, I feel uneasy and I think to myself, "I should be careful today."

14.05 Eating chocolate before an exam, being careful on days when you had a bad dream, not eating seaweed soup before important things. Even if I don't particularly believe in things like that, I still seem to end up following them!

14.06 I'm not particularly superstitious. But if something really did happen relating to a well-known jinx I'd be like "what the heck is going on?" so I guess I worry about them a bit.

14.07 I'm not superstitious. There's a superstition that if you eat seaweed soup on an exam day you'll fail, but I took an exam on my birthday, ate seaweed soup that morning, and I even got a certificate on the exam.

14.08 I am and I'm not. There are times when I pray when faced with something important enough to feel desperate. Psychologically, I think I want to find a place I can lean on. Like religion.

14.09 No, I'm not really superstitious. But there is one thing - it's a correlation between the weather and exams. On past exam days, it rained and those exam grades were good - so if it rains during this exam time as well, I pretty much believe I'm going to have good luck. It just seems to almost always come true!

14.10 All my life I thought I didn't believe in superstitions, but I guess I'm coming to more and more. Not eating seaweed soup on exam days is a given, and I don't sleep with my chair pulled out or anything like that. When arranging your house your mirrors should not face the entryway, you should hide your money and your knives, and you should move on calendar days that end in a zero or a nine.

14.11 I'm not completely superstitious but I don't think there's any harm in not purposely writing names in red or stepping on the threshold of a doorway. This isn't a widely known superstition, but I try to stay balanced on important days, for example on an exam day, if I hold a railing with my left hand, then I'd purposely grab it once with my right hand as well.

15. What are some things you could do to be healthier?

15.01 As soon as I wake up, I follow an eight-minute gymnastics video. Then I wash up and eat an apple for breakfast.

05 번역

15.02 Improving my eating habits. I eat meat-based meals and I need to eat more vegetables.

15.03 I need to try to sleep regularly, exercise consistently, and make an effort to be less stressed.

15.04 I think running is the best. Because in my own personal experience, I've lost quite a bit of weight by running. As we all know, obesity is the enemy of health in all corners of the world.

15.05 I'm currently in Korea in quarantine, but when it ends I intend to get back to exercising. I gained a lot of weight, and before coming to Korea from the US I exercised for about a month and a half and I found getting up in the mornings to be really easy.

15.06 I think messing with my phone less is the most important, on top of that it would be good to exercise every day. Before Corona I exercised every day, but I haven't done it once since. I'm sad because I feel my muscle mass decreasing.

15.07 Proper exercise and proper rest. Also eating many delicious foods... making hobbies just for me... I think each person must relieve stress in their own way. I'm usually a person who relieves stress through food, and these days I'm relieving stress through science fiction or mystery novels.

15.08 I try to do stretches every evening to relieve tension and tiredness in my body and my muscles, but more often than not I forget and don't do it.

15.09 I should probably walk or ride my bike, not just lay at home and watch YouTube, but I feel guilty because I have a mind to do it, but then I just don't follow through.

15.10 In the past I consistently jogged, and on days when I couldn't I went to the mountains or did a few indoor exercises at home. Since I'm lazy, my number one principle is not to go too hard-core. Since I'm not an athlete I don't need to get hung up on records, if it seems a bit too difficult I quit. I want to keep working out every day without giving up and the exercises I like that match that method best are jogging or hiking.

여행

16. What do you mostly do when you're on vacation?

16.01 If it's a place with lots to see, I explore all around, if it's a relaxing resort I hang out at the pool and eat tasty food... in either case I don't miss out, right?

16.02 I like traveling overseas. I stay in cheap B&B's or hostels more than hotels, and I use the money I save for drinking.

16.03 Usually, I like messing around at home. Just chilling without thinking is the best thing for me. You have to give your mind a break, too, right? Haha.

16.04 When I don't have places I 'want to go to' I just stay home. I regret spending my vacation like that, and not traveling around, of course. :'(

16.05 I mostly go traveling, but as I get older I find that going to nearby resorts or staying in at home isn't so bad. Nowadays we can't go out because of Corona, so it's even more so.

16.06 Actually I'm a total homebody and extremely introverted, so on vacation I spend almost all my time at home. Haha. Time flies at home when I binge-watch movies or dramas. Of course if I'm not staying at home, I also go on short trips with friends or family!!

16.07 These days I have fun staycationing at luxury resorts! If it was before Corona I would say I travel overseas, but since the arrival of Corona and this period of social distancing, I've found it's nice to go to a hotel, freely spend time by myself and recharge. It's nice to be able to eat tasty food, take a break, alleviate fatigue, and recharge in a new space!

16.08 Actually, staying home is the best. It's dangerous outside my bed. It's a real vacation when I just cozy up in bed and chill on my phone or laptop, you know? If you're asking about going travelling, I usually go on package trips and just take the bus, go to a tourist spot, take a photo, get back on the bus, go to the next spot, go to a restaurant, go to the bathroom…
it's like being cattle.

17. Where is a place you think everyone should visit?

17.01 America - the place I'm living now. It's a place I think people should visit once in their life.

17.02 Three years ago I did a package tour in Da Nang. I ate a lot of tasty food and the scenery was enjoyable, too. It was too bad I didn't get to try the local street food.

17.03 I don't think I know a place like that, personally. I think it's a big fault of mine that, since I've lived in Korea all my life, I don't see attractive places here as really being attractive.

17.04 I really want to see the Northern Lights. I mean, I should at least record it with my phone and post it on Facebook to brag, right? Haha

17.05 It's not a specific place but I think everyone should go to the Vietnamese fish markets. For our last vacation dinner we went there and it was really fun, it was like catching Pokemon like Ash from Pokemon. Of course, instead of Pokemon, it's fish, and instead of Pokeballs, it's my mouth.

17.06 I totally recommend Gangjin!! Especially for people like me who like to see historical sites - you have to go!! I take my own car so I don't know what the public transport is like, but there're lots of places worth seeing, like Jeong Yak-yong's house of exile, and there's a really cool overall vibe, so it's super memorable.

17.07 As for in Korea, there's a petting zoo near Daegwallyeong sheep ranch! It's a place where you can touch and interact with various animals like ducks, chickens, dogs, horses, sheep, camels, etc. As for overseas, there's a fun place near Kobe, Japan, where you ride a boat on the river with strong winds – it was super memorable.

17.08 If it's Korea, probably Seoul, right? It's the capital so all the things to do and see are bound to be densely packed together. Haha. Even for me, when I want to simply relax I buy a train ticket to Seoul. If not Seoul, then places like Incheon or Busan where there's a big beach or port are fun in a quiet sort of way. As far as overseas goes… I don't have much experience with it so I don't really know :(

17.09 Rome! After I got hired, my company's headquarters were in Rome so I went there for the first time on a business trip. Rome, which I've heard is a must-see attraction, was even more beautiful and attractive in reality. It was so nice to see all the hidden historical sites here and there while wandering the whole city. And the delicious food is a bonus! Haha.

17.10 I haven't been to many places but out of the places I have been to, Busan was the best. It has that vacation-town vibe. If the purpose of the vacation is simply to feel a traditional vibe or just have a quiet break, I really recommend it. Second here is Seoul. Hehe. Additionally, out of the places I haven't been to, I definitely want to go to Jeju Island. All the people around me say that everything there was good. Hehe

17.11 For us people living in a capitalist society, the western culture in the communist country of Cuba is very interesting in several ways. First of all, while the people of Cuba are not materially wealthy, they have a free spirit - an ease that comes from inactivity - which felt odd to me at first, but then my feeling of urgency and impatience left me, and I gradually felt more relaxed. Things that felt worthless in Korea were precious to the locals, and foods and fruits I had never heard of or seen before were commonplace. It is expected that between any countries with different cultural spheres, you will feel some dissonance, but rather than feeling out of place, it felt like a breath of fresh air. They were literally always having family dinners. People say that Cuba is a country where time has stopped, but these days as the internet spreads, there is rapid change centered around the young people.

I like to drink. Cuba's representative alcohol is rum, which is made from fermented sugar cane. The fermented sugar cane is then distilled to make rum, and for me, Havana Club 7-year-old rum is the best. Even now, I cannot forget sitting in Malecon, with the evening breeze blowing and drinking Havana Club. If you have the chance, I definitely recommend going to Cuba.

18. Have you ever travelled somewhere where you didn't speak the language? How did it go?

18.01 I went to Japan and we didn't speak the same language, but the people were so nice and helpful that it was great.

18.02 I went on a trip to South America for a year without knowing Spanish. While there I learned numbers and simple sentences like "It's delicious", "How much is it?", etc. and had a good time.

18.03 Unfortunately, I don't have any overseas travel experience. If I get the chance, I'd like to experience many places like Southeast Asia, the United States, Europe, etc. I'm especially curious about the super sweet fruits in Southeast Asia!

18.04 All the places I've traveled to weren't English speaking countries, so I couldn't communicate well, but if I used body language I could communicate to some extent.

18.05 I've been to Thailand. I could communicate to some extent in simple English, so even without knowing the language I didn't have much trouble. The food was delicious. The weather was very hot, but I expected as much so it was fine. But at times I couldn't pay by credit card, so that was a bit inconvenient.

18.06 Sinuiju City, North Korea, where I went with my aunt. It was a bit off from the standard language, but I knew North Korean from studying during my school days, so fortunately we had no trouble traveling there. My aunt had even lived in North Korea, so I was able to travel more smoothly than ever.

18.07 I have been on a trip to a place where I didn't speak the language. I was filled with worry up until I left, but ultimately once I set off and I came face to face with it I ended up experiencing really fun and enjoyable moments. To make the trip more fun and beneficial I refrained from using English as much as possible.

18.08 I went to Vietnam. I didn't even know how to say hello! But wow, everyone used Korean to the extent that I couldn't tell if it was Korea or Vietnam.. lol Even where that wasn't the case I used simple English and body language to talk.

18.09 Last time I went to Okinawa, Japan and it was ok because I had a guide, but I have an embarrassing memory of going to the convenience store alone and not understanding what the employees said. lol. I think the whole trip was fun because of those kinds of things.

18.10 I went on a trip to Cambodia and China with YellowBalloon. Thanks to their excellent guides both trips had no major problems, but the street vendors were very hard to deal with. We had communication issues - I know I was ripped off by at least 10,000 won. Haha

19. What is your worst vacation memory?

19.01 I went camping during the rainy season, and due to the flooding our tent was washed

번역 05

away by the river.

19.02 I went on a trip to Jeonju and it was just terrible. It's not pretty because there are all kinds of signs hanging on the traditional houses, and the meals were so expensive; I really don't recommend it.

19.03 This reminds me of the time I went on a trip with my girlfriend and we had a big fight, so we just stayed at the hotel all day fuming at each other. :(

19.04 Every time I go to Vietnam I get ripped off. The unit of currency is large so it's difficult to calculate, and Vietnamese merchants always feed on tourists. Of course, I go there often because the food is delicious.

19.05 One time I intended to spend the holiday season spontaneously, but I ended up doing nothing and lying around at home just watching Netflix. Since then, I've been trying to make plans during the holiday season and spend the time a little more wisely.

19.06 When I went to Daecheon in the winter. Nearly 17 hours without sleep + walking in the cold wind on an empty stomach, fighting with my boyfriend... I stayed up all night because of work, so I just kept walking in a daze and couldn't rest. So, I freaked out in the end and exploded.

19.07 Around April I went on a hotel staycation at a luxury resort with a younger student friend I know. I spent a lot more money than my friend, and since we went without making any plans I was so bored. Next time I'm gonna have to bring a movie or something... hahaha

19.08 There was one time where the traffic was bad and I got carsick on the way, so I couldn't even look around properly and I just stayed in the car. But I don't remember how old I was since I was so young.

19.09 I've been so busy and depressed for the last 3~4 years that any vacation was a treat. But when I went to Songdo 2 years ago it rained all day, so that was kind of a shame.

19.10 I think the worst was when I went to Tokyo, Japan. First, all the food I ate then didn't suit my tastes, so while I was in Tokyo, I only ate the hotel breakfasts and I almost starved. :((Strangely, I ate so well when I went to Osaka.... maybe I kept picking the wrong restaurants. :() And then when I went to Disneyland, I even missed the parade while I was on a boring ride. Moreover, the friend I went with kept whining and we had to hurry back to the hotel, so that was a real bummer.

20. Have you ever travelled in first class or business class?

20.1 I never have because I'm a poor traveler. I buy the cheapest plane tickets when I travel, even if I have to stop over somewhere.

20.2 No, I've never even been on a plane before... First class might not be possible, but I'd really like to take my parents on a trip later flying business class. Hehe

20.3 My dad is a pilot! So I've flown a lot ever since I was young. I can count on one hand the number of times I've ridden first class, but I've ridden business class a lot.

20.4 I'd love to fly that way once... I mainly went on backpacking trips, and even when I took a plane I always sat in economy.

20.5 No! But, if I make a lot of money I'd like to try it at least once. I mainly travel abroad to China or Japan, so it only takes 1~2 hours from Incheon International Airport. It's kind of a waste to spend a lot of money on a seat I won't really get to use. ^^;

20.6 Yes, I've ridden them often. I kept ordering grapes and cheese in first class, and since I ordered them up until the stewardess wouldn't give me any more - even when she told me other people need to eat them too - I guess I've also been a bad passenger. If you ride Korean Air, there's a bar behind first class, so they'll make you free cocktails as well. But sadly I quit drinking so I couldn't have any.

20.7 I had to go with my husband to France for 4 months. It was such a long flight, so when I bought the plane tickets I upgraded them to business class. Both times I flew business before were so short, so I hadn't looked around the business compartment properly, but this time I was able to. There was a free bar, the meals were served in courses, and it was full of interesting things! I was even able to sleep with my legs out straight, so I was able to travel really comfortably.

06 어휘

WORD BANK

06 어휘

(배가) 뒤집히다	(a boat) capsizes
(배를) 젓다	to paddle (a boat)
(빵)이 잘 부풀다	the (bread) rises well
(온라인)에 올리다	to post (online)
(총으로) 표적을 겨누다	to take aim at a target (with a gun)
~에게 장난을 치다	to play a joke on
2개국어를 하다	to be bilingual
SNS 중독	a social media addict

ㄱ

가난하다	to be poor
가면 증후군	imposter syndrome
가면무도회	a masquerade
가자미눈하다	to squint when you can't see clearly
가짜 신분증	a fake ID
가짜안경	fake glasses
가창력	singing ability
감사해야 할 일	sth to be thankful for
감소하다	to decrease
감정을 상하게 하다	to hurt sbdy's feelings
감정을 숨기다	to hide feelings
감추다 / 숨기다	to hide / conceal
갓길에 차를 세우다	to pull over to the shoulder
개인적이다	personal / private
거짓말하다	to lie
견인하다	to tow
결정하다	to decide
경복궁	the main royal palace in Seoul
경치	scenery (landscape)
계산하다	to calculate
계좌	bank account
고개를 뒤로 젖히다	tilt one's head back
고민하다	to fret over
고소공포증이 있다	to be afraid of heights
골초	a chain smoker
공군	airforce
공중으로 던지다	to throw in the air
과녁 한가운데에 적중하다	to get a bullseye
과녁을 맞다	to hit the target
과녁을 빗맞다	to miss the target
과소비	overspending
과자	a snack
관광객에게 인기 있다	to be popular with tourists
관광을 하다	to go sightseeing
광고인	an advertiser
교체하다	to replace
구두가 망가지다	to have your shoes break
구두쇠	a miser / cheapskate
구불구불한 길	a winding road
구상하다	to map / plan out
구세주	a savior
국내	domestic
국제	international
군사	military
귀신 나오는 집 / 흉가	a haunted house
귀신을 보다	to see a ghost
귀찮다	to be a pain / to be a drag
균형감각이 좋다	to have a good sense of balance
균형을 잃다	to lose your balance
그건 상황에 따라 달라요.	It depends on the situation.
그나마	even so / nevertheless
그만두다	to quit

어휘 06

극복하다	to overcome
근육	muscle
금식하다	to fast
기계치	sbdy who is technologically challenged
기부하다	to donate
기어를 바꾸다	to shift/change gears
기억에 남다	to be memorable
기온이 영하이다	to have freezing temperatures
기회	an opportunity
긴장성 행동	a nervous habit
길을 잃다	to get lost
길치	sbdy with no sense of direction
깁스를 떼다	to take off a cast
깁스를 하다	to get a cast
까치발로 걷다	to walk on tip-toe
깔끔하다	to be neat / tidy
깨어나다	to wake up (after passing out)
꼬집다	to pinch
꼴등하다	to get last place
꼼꼼하다	to be meticulous
꽃이 피다	the flowers bloom
꾸미다	to decorate
꾸준히	regularly
꿀잼	to be lots of fun (slang)
꿈만 같다	to be like a dream
꿈해몽/꿈풀이	a dream interpretation
꿔다 놓은 보릿자루	sbdy who is 'a stick in the mud'
끔찍하다	to be terrible

ㄴ

나라에 주둔하다	to be stationed in a country
나무젓가락을 쪼개다	to break apart wooden chopsticks
나쁜 특성	a bad trait
나이가 많은 척 하다	to pretend to be older
난폭운전 / 보복운전	road rage
낭만적이다	to be romantic
낭비	a waste
내성적이다	to be introverted
너무 많은 인원들이 나의 관계	to have too many people in your social life
울타리망 속에 있다	to be roomy / spacious
널찍하다	to fall over
넘어지다	to make an effort
노력하다	to be no fun (slang)
노잼	to have an argument
논쟁하다	to tell a joke
농담을 하다	to have/get a black eye
눈에 멍이 들다	to play in the snow
눈에서/눈속에서 놀다	to roll the snow into a snowman
눈을 굴려 눈사람을 만들다	
눈치가 있다	to be aware of social cues

ㄷ

다듬다	to prune
다시마	kelp
단풍이 들다	the leaves change colour
닮다	to resemble
담배를 끊다	to stop smoking
답답하다	to be stuffy / stifling
답사하다/탐험하다	to explore
당구대	a pool table
당구채	a pool cue

06 어휘

당하다	to suffer/undergo sth
당황하다	to be embarrassing
대인관계	interpersonal relations
대판 싸우다	to have a big fight
더 성숙해지다	to become more mature
더위를 먹다 (informal)	to get heatstroke
더위를 식히다	to cool off
덤덤하다	to be thick-skinned
크렌베리	cranberry
도플갱어	doppelganger
독립적이다	to be independent
돈을 걸다	to bet money
돈을 따다	to win woney
돈을 모으다	to save money
돈을 잃다	to lose money
돌아눕다	to turn over
돌아다니다	to wander around
동기	motivation
동작이 우아하다	to have graceful movements
돼지처럼 코를 골다	to snore like a pig
드르렁거리다	to snore (lit. the sound of snoring)
들어눕다	to lie down
들키다	to be caught / found out
따갑다	to feel a stinging feeling on your skin
따돌림 당하다	to be ostracized
딱딱하다	to be firm
딱히 없다	nothing in particular
딸꾹질을 하다	to get hiccups
땀이 나다	to sweat
똑바로 되다	for sth to be done properly
뛰쳐나가다	to storm out

ㄹ	
라이프스타일이 변하다	to transform your life-style
로드트립을 가다	to go on a road trip
리듬감이 좋다	a good sense of rhythm

ㅁ	
마약	drugs
마음대로	as one likes
마음먹다	to decide / to make up your mind
마음속에 그려 보다	to visualize
마음을 새롭게 하다	to freshen your mind
마음이 넓다	to be generous
마취하다	to anesthetize / to put sbdy under
막다	to plug up
막상	actually / ultimately
막힘 없이	without any obstacles
말썽꾸러기	a troublemaker
말을 걸다	strike up a conversation
말이 통하다	to speak the same language
말투	an accent
망망대해	the open sea
머리카락을 잡아당기다	to pull sbdy's hair
멀다	to be far
멀미	motion sickness
멀미약	pills for seasickness
멍때리다	to space out
명소	a sight / attraction
명절 기분을 갖다	to have holiday cheer
모국어	native language
모험을 떠나다	to go on an adventure

207

어휘 06

모험이 되다	to be adventurous
목 근육에 쥐가 나다	to have a crick in one's neck
목이 뻐근하다	to get whiplash
몸치	sbdy who has two left feet
무게	weight
무대 공포증	stage fright
무모하다	to be reckless
무사히	to be safe / without incident
무시하다	to ignore
무의미하다	to be meaningless
무죄를 선고하다	aquit sbdy
무중력	zero gravity
묵다	to stay
문신 가게	a tattoo parlor
문을 두드리다	to knock on a door
문제를 일으키다	to cause trouble
미래를 예언하다	to fortell the future
미루게되다	to put off doing sth
미성년자	a minor (underage)
미식축구	american football
미신에 따르다	according to superstition
미역	seaweed
민망하다	to be embarrassing
믿거나 말거나	believe it or not
믿기지 않다	to be incredible

ㅂ

바가지를 쓰다	to get/be ripped off
바다 생물	sea creatures
바람을 느끼다	to feel the wind
바로	right away
바보 같다	to be a fool
바지가 찢어지다	to have your pants rip
박치	no sense of rhythm
박순이	a party person
발로 차다	to kick
밟다	to step on sth
밤샘 공부하다	to pull an all nighter
방랑자적이다	to be nomadic
방문하다	to visit
방황하다	to feel lost
배경으로 하다	play in the background
배를 타다	to ride a boat
뱉어 내다	to spit sth out
버릇을 고치다	to fix one's habits
범죄를 신고하다	to report a crime
베개	a pillow
벼룩시장	flea market
별명을 부르다	to be called names
별미	a delicacy
별을 보다	to stargaze
별자리	a constellation
보람이 있다	to be worth doing
보충하다	to supplement
보톡스 맞다	to get botox
보험 정보를 교환하다	to exchange insurance information
보호하다	to protect
복용하다	to take a drug / a dose
복잡하다	to be complex / to be crowded
부담이 되다	to be a burden
부지런하다	to be diligent
불만이 있다	to have a complaint
불편하다	uncomfortable / inconvenient
붐비다	to be bustling

06 어휘

브레인스토밍을 하다	to brainstorm
브이로그	a vlog
비사교적이다	to be unsociable
비수기	off-season
비타민제	vitamins
비판을 무시하다	to ignore criticism
비판을 통해 배우다	to learn from criticism
비흡연자	a nonsmoker
빚을 지다	to fall into debt
빨간 불에 지나가다	to run a red light
빨래를 개다	to fold laundry
뺨을 때리다	to slap

ㅅ

사격장	a gun range
사고뭉치	a trainwreck / a walking disaster
사냥총	a hunting gun
사이버 왕따	cyber-bullying
사회 불안	social anxiety
산호초	coral reef
살금살금 가다	to go stealthily
상관없다	to not matter
상금을 타다	to win a prize
상대	the other person
상상하다	to imagine
상징	symbolism
상체 운동	upper body exercizes
상체 힘	upper body strength
상태가 좋다	to be in good shape
색깔을 맞추다	to match colors
생각이 떠오르다	to have thoughts come to your mind
생고기	fresh meat
생생한 상상	a vivid imagination
생활비	living costs
생활비	cost of living
서두르다	to hurry
서로	eachother
서울타워	Seoul Tower
서투르다	to be unskilled
선내	on-board
설명서	instruction guide
설탕 한 숟가락	a spoonful of sugar
섬뜩하다	to be creepy
성수기	peak season
성적 장학금	an academic scholarship
세우다	to set up
소리지르다	to shout
소문이 나다	to have a rumor come out
소문이 내다	to start a rumor
소문이 퍼지다	to have a rumor spread
소비습관	consumption habits
속도 제한	the speed limit
속도위반 딱지를 받다	to get a speeding ticket
속이 울렁거리다	to feel nauseous / queasy
손과 눈을 연결하는 조정력이 좋다	to have good hand-eye coordination
손으로 치다	to punch
손이 크다	to be a big spender
손재주가 있다	to be good with your hands
수다를 떨다	to gossip / to chat
수제품	hand-made items
수집품	a collection
수채화 문신	a watercolour tattoo
숙박	an accomodation
숙취	a hangover

어휘 06

술 깨다	to sober up
술고래	a heavy drinker
술자리	a drinking party
숨을 멈추다 / 참다	to hold one's breath
숨이 멎는 줄 알았다	to be breathtaking
스노보드	snowboard
스스로 하다	to do it yourself
스쿠버 다이빙 자격증	scubadiving certification
스키 점프	ski jump
스키장	ski slope
스트레스 해소	stress relief
스트레스를 풀다	to relieve stress
스트레칭을 하다	to stretch
스페어 타이어	a spare tire
슬금슬금 달아나다	to sneak off
습관을 기르다	to develop a habit
시간을 보내다	to spend time
시동이 걸리다	to restart (the car)
시력검사	an eye test
시력검사판	an eye test chart
식중독	food poisoning
신나다	to be exhilarating
신나다	to be exciting
신선하다	to be fresh
신용카드	a credit card
신체적변화가 있다	to have a physical transformation
실감이 안 나다	to not feel real / to not have sunk in
실천하다	to put one's plan into action
심봤다!	jackpot!
심지어	to even do sth
쓰러지다	to fall over
쓸모있다	to be useful

ㅇ

아무래도 [아무리 생각해도]	somehow / the way I see it...
아쉽다	to be a shame
악보	sheet music
안전하다	to be safe
안타깝다	to be a pity
알딸딸하다	to be buzzed
알뜰하다	to be frugal
앞뒤로 흔들리다	to swing back and forth
애매하다	to be vague / ambiguous / uncertain
앱을 삭제하다	to delete an app
야경	night view
야시장	night market
약속을 어기다	to break a promise
양손잡이다	to be ambidextrous
어디에 있는지 기억을 잘하다	to remember where you've been
어린 척 하다	to pretend to be younger
어색하다	to be awkward
어지럽다	to feel dizzy
어쩔수 없다	it can't be helped
언어 교환	language exchange
얼굴에 달라붙다	to stick to your face
없어지다	to go away / to disappear
엉덩이수술	a boob job
엉뚱하다	to be over the top
엑스레이를 찍다	to get an x-ray
여권	a passport
여러나라	various countries
여울목	(river) rapids
여행 비용	travel expenses
연구하다	to research

연금	a pension
연민을 느끼다	to feel pity
연주회	a recital / performance
열심히	diligently
열정	passion
영감을 받다	to get inspiration
영양가 없는 포스트	a shitpost
영웅	hero
영원히	forever
영향을 주다 / 미치다	to influence sbdy
예민하다	to take things personally
예산을 짜다	to make a budget
예약하다	to book / to reserve
옷에 (물)을 쏟다	to spill (water) on your clothes
외계인을 보다	to see an alien
외롭다	to be lonely
외향적이다	to be extroverted
요리법 / 조리법 / 레시피	a recipe
요리책	a recipe book
용돈	pocket money
우선순위를 매기다	to prioritize
우연히	by accident
우주 비행사	an astronaut
우주선	a space ship
웃기다	to be funny
원하다	to want / wish for
월급	monthly salary
위로가 되다	to be comforting
위험하다	to be dangerous
유명하다	to be famous
유연하다	to be flexible
유적지	historical sights
유죄를 선고하다	convict sbdy
유치하다	to be silly
유행	a fashion trend
으스스하다	to be eerie / spooky
은퇴 계획	a retirement plan
음주운전을 하다	to drink and drive
음질	sound quality
음치	sbdy who is tone deaf
음향	acoustics
의논하다	to discuss
의지력	willpower
이가 고르다	to have straight teeth
이가 비뚤다	to have crooked teeth
인내심	endurance
인정하다	to recognize / acknowledge
일등하다	to get first place
일반학생	an average student
일부러	on purpose
일상 생활	daily life
일상적이다	to be routine / everyday
일정을 지키다	to keep to a schedule
일정을 짜다	to make a schedule
입원하다	to be admitted to the hospital
잊어버리다	to forget
잊을 수 없다	to be unforgettable

ㅈ

자동차	an automatic car
자랑하다	to show off / to brag
자립적이다	to be self-reliant
자유롭게	freely
자존감	self-esteem
자취	living alone
잔액	bank balance
잘 맞다	to match well

어휘 06

잘 어울리다	to be matched well	지니고 다니다	to carry around
잠수복	scubadiving suit	지루하다	to be bored
장화	rain boots	지방 흡입술	to get liposuction
재판	a court trial	지퍼를 잠그다	to have a zipper break
전략적이다	to be strategic	집다	to pick up
전통적인 문신	a traditional tattoo	집에 침입하다	a break-in
절약하다	to save money	짜증이 나다	to be annoyed
접다	to put aside	쫓겨나다	to be thrown out
젓가락질이 서투르다	to be awkward with chopsticks		

ㅊ

차가 멈추다	the car stalls
착각하다	to be mistaken / misunderstand
참다	to endure
창밖을 보다	to look out the window
처방약	prescription drugs
처음으로	for the first time
체육 장학금	a sports scholarship
체크하다	to check off
초대하다	to invite
총기 소지증	a gun license
촬영하다	to film
추천하다	to recommend
축제 현장	a festival venue / site
축하하다	to celebrate
출장	a business trip
충동적이다	to be impulsive
취하다	to be drunk
치유되다	sth heals
친하다	to be friendly
친하다	to be close (emotionally)
칠면조	a turkey
침대 정리하다	to make the bed

정신 건강	mental health
제일 먼저	first of all
제대하다	to be discharged from the army
제외하다	to exclude
조개	a clam
조절하다	to control / regulate
존재하다	to exist
좋은 성적	good grades
좌석을 예약하다	to reserve a seat
죄책감을 느끼다	to feel guilty
주로	mostly / mainly / primarily
주제	theme
주택개조	home improvement
죽을 고비를 넘기다	to have a near-death experience
준비하다	to prepare
줄을 서서 기다리다	to wait in line
중심을 잡다	to keep one's balance
중얼거리다	to mumble
즐기다	to enjoy
증가하다	to increase
지구	earth
지나가는 사람들 구경하기	people-watching

ㅋ

06 어휘

연금	a pension	유행	a fashion trend
연민을 느끼다	to feel pity	으스스하다	to be eerie / spooky
연주회	a recital / performance	은퇴 계획	a retirement plan
열심히	diligently	음주운전을 하다	to drink and drive
열정	passion	음질	sound quality
영감을 받다	to get inspiration	음치	sbdy who is tone deaf
영양가 없는 포스트	a shitpost	음향	acoustics
영웅	hero	의논하다	to discuss
영원히	forever	의지력	willpower
영향을 주다 / 미치다	to influence sbdy	이가 고르다	to have straight teeth
예민하다	to take things personally	이가 비뚤다	to have crooked teeth
예산을 짜다	to make a budget	인내심	endurance
예약하다	to book / to reserve	인정하다	to recognize / acknowledge
옷에 (물)을 쏟다	to spill (water) on your clothes		
외계인을 보다	to see an alien	일등하다	to get first place
외롭다	to be lonely	일반학생	an average student
외향적이다	to be extroverted	일부러	on purpose
요리법 / 조리법 / 레시피	a recipe	일상 생활	daily life
요리책	a recipe book	일상적이다	to be routine / everyday
용돈	pocket money	일정을 지키다	to keep to a schedule
우선순위를 매기다	to prioritize	일정을 짜다	to make a schedule
우연히	by accident	입원하다	to be admitted to the hospital
우주 비행사	an astronaut		
우주선	a space ship	잊어버리다	to forget
웃기다	to be funny	잊을 수 없다	to be unforgettable
원하다	to want / wish for		

ㅈ

월급	monthly salary	자동차	an automatic car
위로가 되다	to be comforting	자랑하다	to show off / to brag
위험하다	to be dangerous	자립적이다	to be self-reliant
유명하다	to be famous	자유롭게	freely
유연하다	to be flexible	자존감	self-esteem
유적지	historical sights	자취	living alone
유죄를 선고하다	convict sbdy	잔액	bank balance
유치하다	to be silly	잘 맞다	to match well

어휘 06

잘 어울리다	to be matched well
잠수복	scubadiving suit
장화	rain boots
재판	a court trial
전략적이다	to be strategic
전통적인 문신	a traditional tattoo
절약하다	to save money
접다	to put aside
젓가락질이 서투르다	to be awkward with chopsticks
정신 건강	mental health
제일 먼저	first of all
제대하다	to be discharged from the army
제외하다	to exclude
조개	a clam
조절하다	to control / regulate
존재하다	to exist
좋은 성적	good grades
좌석을 예약하다	to reserve a seat
죄책감을 느끼다	to feel guilty
주로	mostly / mainly / primarily
주제	theme
주택개조	home improvement
죽을 고비를 넘기다	to have a near-death experience
준비하다	to prepare
줄을 서서 기다리다	to wait in line
중심을 잡다	to keep one's balance
중얼거리다	to mumble
즐기다	to enjoy
증가하다	to increase
지구	earth
지나가는 사람들 구경하기	people-watching
지니고 다니다	to carry around
지루하다	to be bored
지방 흡입술	to get liposuction
지퍼를 잠그다	to have a zipper break
집다	to pick up
집에 침입하다	a break-in
짜증이 나다	to be annoyed
쫓겨나다	to be thrown out

ㅊ

차가 멈추다	the car stalls
착각하다	to be mistaken / misunderstand
참다	to endure
창밖을 보다	to look out the window
처방약	prescription drugs
처음으로	for the first time
체육 장학금	a sports scholarship
체크하다	to check off
초대하다	to invite
총기 소지증	a gun license
촬영하다	to film
추천하다	to recommend
축제 현장	a festival venue / site
축하하다	to celebrate
출장	a business trip
충동적이다	to be impulsive
취하다	to be drunk
치유되다	sth heals
친하다	to be friendly
친하다	to be close (emotionally)
칠면조	a turkey
침대 정리하다	to make the bed

ㅋ

06 어휘

카드 승인이 거절되다	to have your card declined
카드가 한도초과 되다	to exceed your credit limit
카드빚	credit card debt
컴맹	sbdy who is computer illiterate
코고는 사람	a snorer
코수술	a nose job
코스튬을 입다	to wear a costume
크로스컨트리	cross-country skiing
클러치판	the clutch

ㅌ

타투이스트	a tattoo artist
탈수증상	to be dehydrated
터득하다	to get the hang of sth / to have a knack for sth
터지다	to pop
토론하다	to discuss
토하다	to throw up
통제력을 벗어나다	to be out of one's control
퇴원하다	to be discharged from the hospital
퇴직금	severance pay
트레이너	a trainer
특별식	a specialty
특별하다	to be special
특히	especially
(특히) 손으로 만들다	to craft
틈만 나면 하다	to do when you have a chance

ㅍ

파도가 세다	to have strong waves
파산하다	to be bankrupt
파자마 파티	a sleepover
팔꿈치로 치다 / 찌르다	to elbow
패키지 여행	a package trip
팬에 붙다	to stick to the pan
퍼레이드를 보다	to watch a parade
페퍼 스프레이	pepper spray
편안하다	to be comfortable
편집하다	to edit
평범하다	to be ordinary
평행 주차	parallel parking
평화를 찾다	to find peace
폐가	an abandoned house
포장마차	a food stall
포함하다	to include
폭포	a waterfall
푹 쉬다	to get a good rest
품질	quality
풍경	scenery (versatile)
피하다	to avoid
필름이 끊기다	to black out

ㅎ

하룻밤을 보내다	to have a one-night stand
학구적이다	to be academic
한복	traditional korean clothes
한식	korean food
한옥마을	traditional Korean village
할인	a discount
함께 나누다	to share
함부로	recklessly / carelessly
해가 뜨다	the sun rises
해결하다	to solve

어휘 06

해군	navy
해협	a straight / channel
햇살	sunshine
헌혈 운동	a blood drive
헛똑똑이	sbdy who is only "book smart"
헬스 / 헬스장	the gym
헬스하다	to go to the gym
현지인	a local person
혈액형	blood type
혼술하다	to drink alone
화끈거리다	to feel a burning feeling on your skin
화분	a flower pot
확인하다	to check
활로 화살을 한 대 쏘다	to shoot an arrow with a bow
활발하다	to be lively / animated
회의론자	a skeptic
횡설수설하다	to speak gibberish
훈련하다	to train
휘파람으로 곡을 부른다	to whistle a tune
휴게소	a rest stop
흉내내다	to imitate
흉터를 남기다	to leave a scar
흔들리다	to rock / to sway
흡연자	a smoker
힘이 세다	to be strong

www.ingramcontent.com/pod-product-compliance
Lightning Source LLC
Chambersburg PA
CBHW081506080526
44589CB00017B/2668